T0299687

THE
POCKET
GUIDE
TO THE
PATRIARCHY

MAYA OPPENHEIM

PATRIARCHY

(noun)

A system of society or government in which men hold the
power and women are largely excluded from it.

Dedicated to my two grandmas, Joyce Zayne Norris and Hanna Oppenheim – two courageous, determined women who saw the world change profoundly for women during their lifetimes. Hanna, who is 99 and living happily in North London, fled Nazi Germany in 1934 after coming face-to-face with Hitler. Meanwhile, Joyce came to the UK from Jamaica by boat in 1948. Although Joyce is sadly no longer with us, dying after a long battle with Alzheimer's in early 2022, this book is for you both: two women who rebelled against their families to forge their own paths in life when the world was an immensely different place.

First published in Great Britain in 2023 by Trapeze,
an imprint of The Orion Publishing Group Ltd
Carmelite House, 50 Victoria Embankment
London EC4Y 0DZ

An Hachette UK Company

3 5 7 9 10 8 6 4 2

Copyright © Maya Oppenheim 2023

The moral right of Maya Oppenheim be identified as
the author of this work has been asserted in accordance
with the Copyright, Designs and Patents Act of 1988.

All rights reserved. No part of this publication may be
reproduced, stored in a retrieval system, or transmitted
in any form or by any means, electronic, mechanical,
photocopying, recording, or otherwise, without the
prior permission of both the copyright owner and the
above publisher of this book.

A CIP catalogue record for this book is
available from the British Library.

ISBN (Hardback) 978 1 3987 1873 9
ISBN (eBook) 978 1 3987 1874 6
ISBN (Audio) 978 1 3987 1875 3

Printed in Great Britain by Clays Ltd, Elcograf S.p.A

www.orionbooks.co.uk

CONTENTS

INTRODUCTION

There is no shortage of grim stats that elucidate the bleak repercussions of misogyny and gender inequality. As the only women's correspondent at a UK news outlet, I am all too familiar with these facts and figures. Take the statistic that between two and three women are killed by a current male partner or ex-partner every single week in England and Wales,[1] or that a woman is killed by a current or ex-partner with a gun every 16 hours in America.[2] Or that less than 20 per cent of landholders in the world are women.[3] Or that 80 per cent of those displaced by climate change are estimated to be women.[4] Or that in some countries around the world, the legal restrictions on abortions are so stark that women risk long prison sentences – even women who become pregnant after being raped or if her pregnancy has a fatal foetal anomaly or if her health conditions mean she could die from carrying to term or giving birth. Or the fact that roughly 40 per cent of women who are of reproductive age are living somewhere in the world where pregnancy terminations are either illegal or restricted.[5]

Meanwhile, unsafe, backstreet, clandestine abortions are a leading cause of maternal deaths around the world.[6] This is bound to increase substantially in the US, given that the Supreme Court overhauled *Roe vs Wade* – the landmark decision that legalised abortion nationwide in 1973 – in June 2022, with millions of women losing their legal right to have a pregnancy terminated. What's more, let's not forget that around 140 million women are effectively 'missing' around the world due to families choosing to have an abortion as they would prefer to have a son, or not properly caring for a newborn girl.

On top of all this, women are statistically more likely than men to work in low-paid, insecure, precarious forms of employment with zero-hours contracts. They are also far more likely to suffer domestic abuse or sexual violence. The World Health Organization states that one in three women across the world will be forced to endure physical or sexual violence at some point in their lives and it will most likely be perpetrated by a partner.[7] This is unsurprising when 38 per cent of all murders of women around the world are carried out by partners.[8]

In the UK, it is critical to remember just how recently some of the rights women take for granted were introduced. Just a few decades ago, women were in many ways de facto children and second-class citizens in the eyes of the law. Before 1975, women in the UK were barred from opening a bank account in their own name. Moreover, single women were not allowed to submit an application for a loan or a credit card in their own name without getting a signature from their father until the mid-1970s. In the same decade, women were regularly denied mortgages, or were only permitted them if they got a male guarantor to provide a signature. On top of this, women could legally be denied a drink in British pubs until as recently as 1982.

To this very day, women still face a litany of deeply ingrained inequalities in the UK and around the world. Studies have found it is often women who eat 'last and least' in nations wrestling with war or hunger.[9] While in Afghanistan, the Taliban has fiercely escalated restrictions on women's day-to-day freedoms and rights since seizing power of the Afghan capital, Kabul, in mid-August 2021. The group, which previously ruled the country, has blocked women from the workplace, education and public spaces, as well as barring them from taking part in all sports and relinquishing the right to travel alone. But, of course, it is not just women around the world suffering; in a bitterly unequal world where the poorest 50 per cent of the world's population own a meagre 2 per cent of the total net wealth, there are many losers.[10]

Despite the aforementioned grisly statistics, there is still a shocking number of men, and some women, too, who will tell you sexism and misogyny no longer exist, and that things are now equal for men and women. Whether it is the performative woke bloke who suddenly reveals himself to be a rampant misogynist or the well-meaning but know-it-all uncle who keeps saying things that make your skin crawl, so many of us have experienced those frustrating moments when your experience is denied and you can't find the words to challenge it. So how do you stand up to those folks who are in denial that misogyny exists? Well, this book – which is replete with clear data, digestible bite-sized gems, campaigning resources and thought-provoking quotes – is a good place to start.

The Pocket Guide to the Patriarchy will show you, and help you show others, how different elements of the patriarchy are connected, and what we can – and must – do to tackle this.

In this book I will shine a glaring, unflinching hydroponic light on the injustice suffered by so many women and people of marginalised genders. And in the same way that hydroponic lights help plants to grow, I hope this guide will help you expand your own understanding, and in doing so help others grow some requisite knowledge, so the seeds are planted for a better future. In each chapter I share important statistics, and in some I share wins and developments that have been made. Not every chapter has wins listed because in certain areas I felt there was a dearth of significant and enduring breakthroughs.

On a separate note, it is worth bearing in mind the issues explored in this book impact the lives of women, trans, non-binary and gender diverse individuals. Women are not the only individuals who menstruate, give birth, have abortions or experience harassment, violence or economic insecurity and the topic matters we will go on to explore have crippling repercussions on gender diverse individuals too. While gender diverse people are not always explicitly mentioned throughout the book, their experiences must not be discounted or overlooked. What's more, it must also be remembered the patriarchy does not serve all men equally and its structures inflict harm on them too.

Knowledge is important, as it is so often the people who have done the least homework who shout the most aggressively that gender inequality is all but a myth. This suspicious, incredulous view of gender inequality is rife in far-right circles. So as the far right grows – restyling and sugar-coating itself but retaining and even bolstering its destructive fascist ideals – the more people inside and outside the movement seem to adopt this perspective.

It is no secret that the fight for women's rights, trans rights and gender equality has become a key casualty in the repugnant ramping-up of the so-called 'culture wars'. But what exactly are the 'culture wars'? At first glance, the phrase, which routinely pops up in headlines, might sound like a synonym for Mariah Carey versus Mozart, or Tolstoy versus *10 Things I Hate about You*, but 'culture wars' are not a reference to purported 'low' versus 'high' culture. On the contrary, the Cambridge Dictionary defines culture wars as 'disagreements about cultural and social beliefs between groups, especially between people with more conservative opinions and people with more progressive opinions'.

In some ways the culture wars are caricatures of a certain set of values, as well as a modern manifestation of the historic division between right- and left-wing politics. Those on the conservative side of the culture wars often promote traditional notions of the family, take an essentialist, biologically deterministic view of gender and resist notions of structural racism, as well as taking a traditionalist and perhaps nationalist approach to society, which glorifies the past and dismisses emotional sensitivity from so-called 'snowflakes'. Those on the progressive side, meanwhile, may be more cosmopolitan, metropolitan, permissive, tolerant, emotionally open, and have a critical understanding of race and a non-essentialist view of gender, which champions the rights of different gender identities. However, there are of course nuances, grey areas and exceptions to these broad-stroke examples of the dividing lines.

The explosion of the culture wars, no doubt fuelled by provocative, opportunistic, divisive politicians, is part and parcel of a growing backlash against feminism, with the grim term 'feminazis' slung around men's rights circles online more and more, and the realities of women's experience minimised and weaponised against us.

With all that in mind, this is a book to arm you with the facts and real-world stories to tell your friends and foes why we have much further to go to extricate and liberate women from inequality and injustice.

'77%

OF ANTI-ABORTION LEADERS ARE MEN.

100%

OF THEM WILL NEVER BE PREGNANT.'

PRO-CHOICE PUBLIC EDUCATION

PROJECT CAMPAIGN

1

ABORTION

'I am no longer accepting the things I cannot change.
I am changing the things I cannot accept.'

Angela Davis

There is arguably no issue in mainstream political discourse as viciously polarising as abortion rights. This is because on one side you have people who think women who have abortions are murderers and on the other side you have people who think women should be able to decide whether or not they continue with a pregnancy. Unsurprisingly, it is hard for these two groups to find middle ground or compromise. If you believe abortion is not only a safe, routine and legal form of healthcare, but also an indispensable human right, it is hard to engage with someone who sees pregnancy terminations as akin to murder. If you want to get a sense of the graphic and disturbing language employed by those who are against abortion, then you need look no further than Jacob Rees-Mogg, a senior Conservative Party MP, who branded abortions morally wrong and a 'cult of death', arguing that they should not even be allowed in instances where the pregnancy was the result of rape or incest.

Another key difference between the anti-abortion movement and other forms of campaigning is that anti-abortion activists do not direct their efforts at the government, big business or fossil fuel companies; instead, they target patients seeking healthcare as well as the nurses and doctors providing it. Irrespective of the fact that whether or not to have an abortion can be one of the most difficult decisions of someone's life, anti-abortion ideologues will harass women seeking abortions outside clinics.

Disturbing views pushed by anti-abortion activists span from linking abortion to satanism, the devil and child sacrifice, to being opposed to sex and birth control, to believing pregnancy terminations should be banned in cases of rape. Experts have told me that the majority of anti-abortion activists in the UK are opposed to abortions in instances of rape, incest, fatal foetal abnormality or if the pregnancy places the woman's life at risk.[11]

Harassment tactics routinely employed by such activists include yelling 'mum' or 'murderer' at women outside clinics, distributing medically erroneous pamphlets (such as material which falsely claims abortions give you breast cancer), following women down the street and much more. This is not a fringe issue; more than 100,000 women are estimated to have attended clinics targeted by anti-abortion demonstrations in 2019.[12] However, fortunately it is now illegal for protesters to employ these tactics outside abortion clinics, with MPs voting in favour of nationwide 'buffer zones' outside services that provide terminations in England and Wales in autumn 2022. For the record, a 'buffer zone' stops anti-abortion protesters or any other type of demonstrator standing outside the clinic or hospital or in the near vicinity.

It would be a mistake to assume that religiosity goes hand in hand with anti-abortion activism. Surveys of British social attitudes demonstrate that people of faith are almost as likely to believe that women should have the right to choose an abortion as non-religious individuals. Moreover, polling released in 2020 found that nine in ten UK adults think women should be able to access abortion services in Britain and specifically identify as being 'pro-choice'.[13] This is a relief when you consider that around one in three women in Britain will have an abortion in their life.

While abortion has long been legal in the UK, sadly this is not the case in many countries around the world where the procedure remains against the law and those who obtain a termination or provide one face a fine or prison time. The data is crystal clear: banning abortions does not stop terminations from taking place; it just pushes the procedures underground, forcing women to have dangerous, illegal, clandestine abortions instead. Unsafe abortion remains a major – yet wholly preventable – cause of maternal deaths and health complications around the world. Research by the United Nations Population Fund has found that over 60 per cent of unintended pregnancies result in an abortion, while an estimated 45 per cent of all abortions around the world are dangerous. Researchers noted that some 5–13 per cent of all maternal deaths are the by-product of unsafe backstreet abortions.[14] The pregnancy terminations are carried out in contexts where abortion is illegal, highly restricted or too expensive to afford. Women are not the only people who have abortions, with trans men and non-binary people also seeking pregnancy terminations and facing additional stigma while doing so.

In short, banning abortion is highly dangerous for the health of women and people with wombs. What's more, reducing access to safe abortions hits women in marginalised and poor communities, as well as those in remote, rural areas, the hardest. This is becoming a growing problem in the US in the wake of the Supreme Court dismantling *Roe vs Wade* – the landmark decision that legalised abortion nationwide in 1973 – in June 2022. While fierce debates about abortion have long raged in America, Donald Trump's arrival into the White House in January 2017 emboldened anti-abortion ideologues to new zeniths. But most significantly, the former US president appointed the Supreme Court justices who went on to reverse *Roe vs Wade*. Abortion access across vast chunks of America has changed beyond recognition since *Roe* was overturned, with millions of women losing their legal right to have an abortion and most pregnancy terminations banned in 13 states. In Georgia, abortions are banned at around the six-week mark of pregnancy – a point at which many women have no idea they are pregnant. This begs the question: how can you know if you want an abortion, or request one from healthcare services, if you don't even know you are pregnant in the first place? On top of this, most of the US states who have rapidly curtailed abortion in the wake of *Roe*'s overturning have chosen not to allow pregnancy terminations in cases of rape or incest.

Abortion pills have also been caught up in the war on reproductive rights. Matthew Kacsmaryk, a Trump-appointed conservative US district judge in Texas, ruled against medical abortions across the US in April 2023 – suspending the Food and Drug Administration's 20-year approval of the abortion drug mifepristone. However, in the space of just minutes, a different district judge issued the polar opposite ruling in the state of Washington. Joe Biden's administration has promised to challenge Kacsmaryk's ruling. The debacle was triggered by a group of anti-abortion activists and a right-wing legal group launching legal action to overturn the federal government's approval of Mifepristone. In turn, Kacsmaryk acquiesced, precipitating a legal challenge that is likely to wind up at the US Supreme Court. Having a medical abortion involves taking two tablets, with mifepristone being the first. Medical abortions constitute more than half of all abortions in America and mifepristone has been used by millions of women around the world to terminate their unwanted pregnancy.[15]

If there is one tiny sliver of a silver lining to the sinister situation engulfing America, it is the fact that it has shone a light on issues with abortion access across the pond in the UK. Somewhat staggeringly, abortions are still deemed a criminal act in England, Scotland and Wales under the 1967 Abortion Act. Legislation passed in 1861 means that any woman who ends a pregnancy without getting legal permission from two doctors, who must agree that continuing with it would be risky for the woman's physical or mental health, can face up to life imprisonment. Any medical professional who delivers an abortion out of the terms of the Act can face criminal punishment.

Even though abortion providers, charities, prestigious medical bodies, MPs and campaigners have spent years demanding that abortion be decriminalised in the UK, it continues to be an issue many remain unaware of. Extricating abortion law from a criminal framework also does not look like something the current Conservative government is particularly eager to do. I have reported on records which show that the current UK prime minister, Rishi Sunak, and senior members of his government have voted against boosting access to abortions or have opted out of key votes on terminations.[16]

All this injustice around abortions is, in part, born out of misogynistic misconceptions, which not only reduce women to wombs with legs, but also overlook the manifold reasons why you might choose to have an abortion. These include, but are not limited to, not wanting a child, not being able to afford to have a child, already having lots of kids and not wanting more, the pregnancy taking place in the context of rape or domestic abuse, having a fatal foetal abnormality or having a health issue that means carrying a pregnancy to term could result in your own death.

Abortion is a topic I feel deeply passionate about and one that I have direct experience of. In spring 2022, I wrote a first-hand story detailing my nightmare struggle to access an abortion earlier that same year. Overwhelmed, overstretched abortion services meant that it was suggested I travel hundreds of miles from the capital of London, where I live, to Doncaster or Liverpool.[17] If this wasn't bad enough, delays meant I was pushed to the point of nearly needing to have a surgical abortion instead of a medical one. Even though such procedures are safe, they are far riskier for your health, and more invasive, too. The article explains in detail the process of having an abortion so may be helpful for anyone going through it themselves, or for a loved one supporting them.

The people out there who are opposed to abortions are entitled to their viewpoint but should not feel they have a right to force their own personal perspective and agenda onto other people's bodies and lives. Forcing, pushing or coercing women to continue with an unwanted pregnancy is akin to torture. Take the recent case of an American woman on holiday in Malta seeking an abortion. Malta has one of the most stringent anti-abortion laws in the world with terminations illegal in all contexts. This woman experienced doctors refusing her a potentially life-saving abortion after she went to hospital with severe bleeding at 16 weeks pregnant. Her anguish and the alleged zero chance of her baby surviving did not spur them to help her. You see, anti-abortion ideologues hark on about being 'pro-life', but this purported interest in 'life' feels hollow and disingenuous when they give little consideration to the life of the woman carrying the baby. Surely, she should have the final say.

THE STATS

> Abortion pills have been prohibited altogether or access to them has been restricted in almost half of US states.[18]

> More countries are adopting policies that coerce women into having more children, with 'right-wing, populist and nationalist administrations stigmatising women who choose to have smaller families as unpatriotic'.[19]

> Around a third of women in the UK do not know how to get an abortion where they live, while only one in four people understands how the law on abortion works in the UK.[20]

> UK Prime Minister Rishi Sunak, Chancellor Jeremy Hunt, Foreign Secretary James Cleverly and Home Secretary Suella Braverman have abstained or voted against all English abortion legislation since 2015 – including moves to roll out 'buffer zones' around abortion clinics to protect women seeking terminations from being harassed by protesters, to allow at-home early medical abortions and to decriminalise terminations.[21]

> The UK's largest study into abortions found at-home early medical abortions pose no greater risk and allow women to have the procedure much earlier on in their pregnancy.[22]

> Increasing numbers of Britons have been investigated by police over suspected illegal abortions.[23]

> Rates of unintended pregnancies are steepest in nations where abortion access is curbed, yet lowest in countries where pregnancy terminations are lawful.[24]

> Abortion rates are similar in nations where pregnancy terminations are curbed to those in countries where they are legal.[25]

> Over 22,000 women and girls are estimated to die every year in the wake of a dangerous pregnancy termination.[26]

> Millions of women and girls are forced to go to hospital every year due to complications which arise from dangerous

abortions – with some left disabled, or not able to get pregnant again.[27]

> Transgender, non-binary and gender-diverse people accessing abortions face barriers and stigma due to facing transphobia and ignorance from healthcare providers.

> There are total abortion bans in the Philippines, the Dominican Republic, Egypt, Iraq, Laos, Nicaragua, El Salvador, Honduras, Senegal and Haiti among other countries.[28]

> Around three dozen different nations only permit abortions in instances where the woman's life is at risk, including Mexico, Nigeria, Iran, Brazil, Venezuela, Myanmar and Afghanistan.[29]

THE WINS

> Termination of pregnancies became legal in Northern Ireland in October 2019 after MPs in Westminster voted by a landslide to give women the right to abortion – marking an end to the procedure being banned in almost all circumstances, even rape and incest.

> After Covid hit the UK in March 2020, ministers allowed abortion pills to be sent via post to be taken at home after a phone consultation.

> MPs voted in favour of nationwide 'buffer zones' outside abortion clinics in England and Wales – with a so-called buffer zone stopping anti-abortion protesters or any other types of demonstrators standing outside the clinic or hospital or in the near vicinity.

> Mexico's Supreme Court ruled in 2021 that criminal penalties for having a pregnancy terminated were unconstitutional.

> Argentina became the first major Latin American country to legalise abortion in December 2020, representing a major victory for feminist activists who had been striving to overhaul highly restrictive abortion laws for over three decades.

> In 2022 Colombia became the latest country in Latin America to decriminalise abortion.

RESOURCES

> British Pregnancy Advisory Service (BPAS) and MSI Reproductive Choices UK – UK's two leading abortion providers.

> Women on Web – online abortion service supporting people to access safe abortion pills in nearly 200 countries, including those where abortion is illegal or restricted.

> Doctors for Choice – coalition of doctors, healthcare workers, and students campaigning for abortion rights.

> Abortion Support Network – enabling people to access abortions in Poland, France, Hungary, Ireland, Spain, Northern Ireland and other EU countries.

> Abortion Rights – prominent national pro-choice campaigning organisation.

> Guttmacher Institute – research organisation championing sexual and reproductive health and rights around the world.

> Ipas – advancing reproductive justice by expanding access to abortion and contraception.

> Planned Parenthood – largest US abortion and reproductive healthcare provider also working globally.

2

DOMESTIC ABUSE

'Men are afraid that women will laugh at them.
Women are afraid that men will kill them.'

Margaret Atwood

Most criminals do not tell their victims they love them. Most crimes are perpetrated outside of the home. Most victims do not love the person who is perpetrating the crimes against them. But domestic abuse is not like other crimes and has a higher rate of repeat victimisation than any other.[30]

A woman will attempt to escape a violent partner an average of seven times before she finally manages to flee. But just because she has left does not mean she is safe. Statistics show that women are at high risk of being murdered by their ex-partner when they gather the courage to escape and are routinely killed in the first month or year after having fled.[31]

The data also shows that between two and three women are killed by a current male partner or ex-partner every single week in England and Wales, while one in four women is estimated to suffer domestic abuse at some point during their life.[32] Despite this, women killed in domestic homicides are routinely overlooked by society, or, worse still, blamed for their own murder.

Take the unshakeably brutal murder of a beautiful young woman called Ingrid Escamilla who was stabbed to death by her partner in Mexico in 2020. Leaked images of her mutilated body were splashed on the front page of the Mexican newspaper *Pasala* alongside the caption: 'It was Cupid's fault.' Ingrid had her organs and skin removed – a sick and twisted act that most would not associate with Cupid or love. Her partner, who was covered in blood sitting in a police vehicle, was captured on camera telling the police he had stabbed her after they'd had a fight over his drinking and had binned her body parts in the drainage.

And if you want more proof of how people attempt to normalise domestic abuse or act like male violence is the ultimate display of love, take the traditional Russian saying: 'If he beats you, it means he loves you.' While fortunately there is no mantra quite as disturbing in the UK, the notion that domestic abuse is somehow a crime of frenzied romantic passion is deeply ingrained within our society, too.

Domestic abuse is all about control. The one thing most domestic abusers have in common is a desire to have power and authority over their victims. Research shows that domestic homicides often follow a lengthy, torturous campaign of domestic abuse.[33] And then their death is the abuser enacting the darkest and of course most irreversible form of control: ending their life.

This raises the question of what exactly domestic abuse is. Many victims say it is akin to being in prison. Domestic abuse is characterised by some or all of the following: coercive control, emotional abuse, psychological manipulation, sexual violence, financial abuse and physical violence. Having interviewed scores of domestic abuse survivors, as well as adults who grew up in households where domestic abuse was present, and frontline workers who support victims fleeing abusive partners, I have found that parallels between different abusers do start to emerge.

Domestic abuse victims often do not initially realise they are in an abusive relationship. This is because abuse often slowly builds up and intensifies as the relationship progresses. This can involve partners telling you what to wear and who to be friends with, guilt-tripping you for socialising, never taking responsibility or apologising for wrongdoing, being overly possessive and jealous, and hurling verbal abuse in arguments, which they then downplay and minimise. However, domestic abuse also manifests in starker ways. Take the woman I interviewed whose ex-partner would routinely beat her up, confiscate her bank card and keys, lock her in the house and destroy her SIM cards.[34] Her abusive ex-partner once strangled her while she was holding her baby – an image that is hard to shake from your mind. The woman in question was forced to move 11 times to escape this violent person. This type of behaviour might sound extreme and dark, which of course it is, but sadly it is also run-of-the-mill for many perpetrators. And the data shows that many domestic abusers are serial perpetrators, having abused multiple women.

Laura Richards, a former top Metropolitan Police violent crime analyst, explained through her research she has found domestic abusers and sexual offenders are often serial perpetrators and offend both inside and outside the home. 'Police and others need to be proactive in their investigations and make the links across public protection to better protect women and children,' Richards, also former head of the Sexual Offences Section & Homicide Prevention Unit and founder of anti-stalking charity Paladin, told me.

'MEN ARE AFRAID THAT WOMEN WILL LAUGH AT THEM. WOMEN ARE AFRAID THAT MEN WILL KILL THEM.'

MARGARET ATWOOD

The more interviews I have done with survivors of unspeakable domestic abuse, the more I have realised how common the aforementioned anecdotes are. Men threatening to kill their partners. Men routinely ringing their girlfriends or wives 50 times a day to check up on what they are doing. Perpetrators trawling through a girlfriend's phone without permission or relentlessly accusing them of being gay for simply spending time with their female friends, or isolating them from relatives, friends, colleagues or neighbours.

The stories I hear are sickening. The kinds of things that make you do a double take. The kinds of things you initially think you misheard. Men slashing their ex's car tyres or smashing their windows in. Obliterating their homes like a literal bull in a china shop. Men who expect and force their victims to do all the cleaning and who shout if they don't do it right. Men who ban their partners from working. Hot-tempered, belligerently entitled men, with egos more fragile than glass baubles, who subscribe to a highly misogynistic world view where the role of the girlfriend or wife is simply to serve their every wish. Men who have a prescriptive, rigid yet delusional paranoid idea about what a girlfriend is and isn't allowed to do. Who have a tacit or explicit rulebook their partner has to live by.

So who are these perpetrators? It is no exaggeration to say that many of these men are highly dangerous individuals. After all, there is a reason why domestic abuse refuges, which house many women at risk of murder if they stay with their violent partner, are situated in highly secret locations with no letter box and stringent security measures to make sure the victims living there are not in danger. I remember accidentally walking past Reigate and Banstead Women's Aid refuge in Surrey initially, which I visited to interview survivors, due to its inconspicuous location.

Getting a place in a shelter for domestic abuse victims has become increasingly difficult in recent years, however, as refuges have seen their funding decimated due to austerity measures, with many forced to close or cut their services altogether. As a direct consequence, those in need of a refuge to escape their abuser are being pushed into homelessness or forced to risk their safety by returning to their abuser, where they face further torment. This, and more, is why domestic abuse survivors routinely tell me that the system for seeking justice against their perpetrator is broken. You hear of women whose exes are released on bail within viewing distance of their homes or, worse still, released to the home they shared together.

It is worth noting women and gender-diverse individuals are not the only ones who are subjected to domestic abuse and it is an issue which can also be experienced by men. Nevertheless, leading UK organisations in this sector do consider domestic abuse to be a 'gendered crime', arguing while it is experienced by both men and women, it is women who are substantially more likely to endure severe and recurrent forms of abuse and violence, including ill-treatment which is sexual. Such organisations also note women are more likely to be subjected to domestic abuse which leads to injuries, or sees them murdered, as well as considering violence against women to have its roots in wider gender inequality.

Domestic abuse remains an acutely misunderstood phenomenon, with victims forced to battle guilt, blame and shame, and routinely interrogated about why they wouldn't simply pack up and leave their abuser. The question 'Why don't women leave?' might not be asked as explicitly as it was years ago, but it is still frequently alluded to. This is despite the fact that it fails to recognise the dynamics of domestic abuse, overlooking the reality that victims may feel too scared to leave, may not be able to afford to flee due to suffering financial abuse, or may have been so worn down by abuse that their mental health is in tatters. What's more, they may have been so isolated by their abuser that they have nobody to turn to, or so badly manipulated that they do not realise they are being abused, as well as countless other barriers. To put it simply: abusers often strive to take away your past by isolating you from those who surrounded you before they came along, slyly turning you against your nearest and dearest by making you believe that they don't genuinely care about you. Then they endeavour to ruin your present by obliterating your freedom and happiness, and seek to destroy your future by inflicting trauma on you.

Domestic abuse ruins lives, but at its worst it ends lives. After all, that is what is at stake in these situations: a human life. The women who are killed year in, year out in the UK by current or former partners are not just grisly statistics; they are daughters, mothers, best friends, grandmothers, aunts, ex-wives, ex-girlfriends, old flames, colleagues and acquaintances. Women who have had their lives and dreams stolen from them. Women whom other human beings love and depend on, and whose deaths leave behind the toxic debris of trauma.

THE STATS

> Between two and three women are murdered each week by their partners or ex-partners in England and Wales.[35]

> A woman will attempt to escape an abusive partner an average of seven times before she manages to flee.[36]

> Police in England and Wales receive an average of over 100 calls an hour on domestic abuse across a year.[37]

> Professor Evan Stark, a prominent coercive control expert who coined the term, compares coercive control to being

taken hostage. In his own words: 'The victim becomes captive in an unreal world created by the abuser, entrapped in a world of confusion, contradiction and fear.'[38]

> Although domestic abuse transcends class, age, race, sexuality, migration status and disability, some groups experience violence at the hands of their partner at higher rates than others. Women with disabilities, for example, are more than twice as likely to be victims of domestic violence and to endure it for longer stretches of time than able-bodied women.[39]

> Calls to the national domestic abuse helpline skyrocketed by 22 per cent in the year ending March 2021.[40]

> Research has found that domestic abuse can affect an individual's physical health, with women who have suffered from it 44 per cent more likely to die from any cause than the wider population. The same research also found that domestic abuse survivors were at an increased risk of developing cardiometabolic diseases such as Type 2 diabetes and cardiovascular disease.[41]

> Reports of domestic abuse and sexual violence against transgender and non-binary people surged by 18 per cent between the years 2020/21 and 2021/22, data shows.[42]

> One in five women murdered by a partner formerly had contact with the police.[43]

THE WINS

> Coercive control became a specific offence in England and Wales in 2015, and awareness of the non-violent elements of domestic abuse has grown in the years since.

> The Domestic Abuse Bill was passed in the UK in 2021, with the landmark legislation stopping perpetrators from cross-examining victims in family courts, ending the so-called 'rough sex' defence and criminalising threats to share revenge porn. The bill also implemented the first ever statutory definition of domestic abuse to encompass financial abuse and controlling, manipulative behaviour.

> Pharmacies and TSB banks joined forces with the government in 2021 to launch a codeword scheme, which provided a 'lifeline' to domestic abuse victims struggling during lockdown. The scheme is still in place.

> A scheme called Rail to Refuge was launched in March 2020, which gives domestic abuse survivors a free train ticket to escape abusive partners and seek refuge in a shelter.

> A silver lining to the pandemic is that awareness of domestic abuse has risen around the world.

RESOURCES

> Refuge – a leading domestic abuse charity which is England's largest provider of shelters for domestic abuse victims.

> Women's Aid – another leading domestic abuse charity.

> National Domestic Abuse Helpline – run by Refuge and open 24/7, 365 days per year, on 0808 2000 247 or through nationaldahelpline.org.uk.

> Level Up media guidelines for reporting on domestic abuse.

> Sistah Space – London's only domestic abuse service for African- and Caribbean-heritage women.

> IMKAAN – umbrella organisation dedicated to addressing violence against black and minoritised women and girls.

> Galop – helping LGBT+ individuals who have endured violence and abuse.

> Surviving Economic Abuse – unique UK charity which tackles financial abuse.

> Respect – leading domestic abuse charity which helps deliver perpetrator programmes and runs a helpline for perpetrators to call.

> The Freedom Programme – scheme predominantly created for female domestic abuse survivors.

> National Centre for Domestic Violence – provides free emergency injunctions for abuse survivors.

3

PERIODS

'What would happen, for instance, if suddenly, magically, men could menstruate and women could not? The answer is clear – menstruation would become an enviable, boast-worthy, masculine event: Men would brag about how long and how much.'

Gloria Steinem

Throughout history, periods have been cloaked in stigma, shame and disgust. There are as many layers to this deeply entrenched taboo as there are brands of period products. At its darkest, the taboo around periods puts lives and health at risk. Take the dozens of women and girls who have died in Nepal in recent years as a direct result of an ancient tradition that banishes menstruating women to outside huts or sheds for animals.[44] When you bear in mind that temperatures in Nepal sometimes plummet to below zero in the winter months, you can understand why this is such a grim prospect. The practice also involves women being banned from partaking in family activities and coming into contact with men and being given less food while on their periods. The most common way to die is from inhaling smoke from the fire you have been forced to start to stop yourself from freezing to death, but, sadly, other women and girls have died after being attacked by wild animals. While the ancient Hindu practice known as 'chhaupadi' has technically been banned since the mid-noughties, it continues to remain pervasive in some areas of western Nepal.[45] Women who are married can generally get away with staying outside for just a few days, but others can be temporarily extradited outdoors for up to an entire week. In other words, women and girls spend a hefty chunk of their lives being ejected from their homes.

Hundreds of thousands of miles away in the UK, the taboo around periods continues. Until the beginning of 2021, sanitary products in the UK were deemed to be 'luxury, non-essential' items and were taxed at 5 per cent. But while 5 per cent of tax might seem a little steep, it is a good deal cheaper than the extortionate 17.5 per cent rate at which sanitary items were taxed prior to 2001. If this means nothing to you, think about the fact that exotic meats like crocodile and kangaroo, Jaffa Cakes and alcoholic jellies are deemed to be essential items and are thus not taxed at all. To put it simply, having a period is expensive: the average lifetime cost of forking out on period products and other items to make your period more bearable is estimated to be over £18,000 per person.[46] These extra products predominantly consist of period items themselves, fresh replacement pants and pain-relief tablets.

As such, it is no surprise that period poverty is a massive problem around the world. As many as three in ten girls in the UK struggled to afford or access period products during the coronavirus pandemic, with over half of them having to resort to using toilet paper instead of proper products.[47] Meanwhile, around the world the situation is stark, with at least 500 million women and girls not having access to the facilities they require for their periods, the World Bank estimates, while as many as 1.25 billion women and girls are unable to access a toilet that is 'safe' and 'private'.[48] This is an issue that can have troubling mental health repercussions, with studies finding that women who have suffered period poverty are more likely to contend with anxiety or depression.[49]

The situation is much worse for those living in countries where totally baseless, ludicrous myths about periods persist. Plan International probed girls and its own staff around the world about some of the common myths about periods, and the findings were jaw-dropping.[50] In Colombia, periods can stop women from cooking, cleaning, harvesting, carrying babies, touching plants or doing sports. In Cameroon, some think you should steer clear of washing in rivers, going fishing, eating meat or going near fresh crops while menstruating, with women sometimes barred from holding a baby who is up to three months old. And some think women on their periods must climb out of the window when entering or leaving the house. In Guinea, some people bar girls from attending school while menstruating. And in Senegal, it is thought that if you let someone who is menstruating use an open well, it could dry out or instead be filled with blood. Granted, here in the UK bizarre yet damaging myths around periods are less prevalent, but menstruation remains plagued with stigma.

There are many reasons why the taboo around periods strikes me as strange. One is due to their sheer ubiquity. Why are we in denial about something that half of the population of the world goes through each month for a large chunk of their lives? Some wise words, said by my ever sagacious and astute 99-year-old grandma, spring to mind: 'There is no point in arguing about the things you do regularly in life.' While this no doubt sounds like good advice for anyone who has been in a relationship of any kind, it may strike you as irrelevant, tangential advice for menstruation. But the justification of why we need to smash the taboos around periods to smithereens rests on a similar premise: why shroud the omnipresent, universal and scientifically necessary experience of bleeding each month in shame?

Men, friends, colleagues, hobbies, brain cells and socks have come and gone since the sunny day in Essex back in the early noughties when I bled for the first time, but my periods have remained a constant. To adapt an overused adage from Benjamin Franklin, one of the Founding Fathers of the US of A, from way back in 1789: nothing is certain in life except death, taxes (and periods).

THE STATS

› A woman menstruates for an average of around seven years in her entire life.[51]

› Poor menstrual hygiene puts physical health at risk and can cause reproductive and urinary tract infections.[52]

› Sanitary products were taxed at a whopping 17.5 per cent prior to 2001 (meanwhile, exotic meats like crocodile and kangaroo are deemed essential items and not taxed at all).

› More than a quarter of women say they were forced to miss work or school due to not being able to afford period products in England, Scotland and Wales.[53]

› More than a third of girls and young women in the UK struggled to afford or access period products in the Covid-19 crisis.[54]

> One in five girls and young women in the UK has been teased or bullied because of their periods.[55]

> Toxic shock syndrome, which can be triggered by leaving a tampon in for too long, is a rare condition, but while it leads to very few deaths worldwide per year, it can cause serious chronic and irreversible conditions, like limb amputation.

> Some 500 million women and girls around the world are estimated not to have access to period products and services to safely manage their periods.[56]

> According to one study, almost a quarter of young people in the UK would brand periods embarrassing and a fifth would call them 'gross'. The same study discovered that almost one in four girls and young women say they didn't know what was going on when their periods began.[57]

THE WINS

> Japan became the first country to give leave to female employees with period pains back in 1947.

> The UK government set up a specific taskforce dedicated to ending period poverty in 2019.

> Girls at primary and secondary schools in England and Wales were given free sanitary products from early 2020.

> The UK government announced the Tampon Tax Fund back in 2015, in which money from taxes amassed from period products was used to 'fund women's health and support charities'.

> Scotland became the first country in the world to provide free period products in November 2020.

> The UK's Tampon Tax was scrapped at the beginning of 2021.

> Several states in America have passed laws mandating that free period products are delivered in schools.

> Several countries and US states reduced or altogether axed taxes on period products, including Australia, Canada, Colombia, Kenya, Australia, India, Malaysia, Nicaragua, Jamaica, Lebanon, Nigeria, Trinidad and Tobago, and Uganda.

> At the beginning of 2023, Spain became the first European country to pass legislation permitting individuals with painful periods to take paid 'menstrual leave' from the workplace – with the government funding the policy.

RESOURCES

> Bloody Good Period – a charity that supplies menstrual products to people in need in the UK.

> Binti Period – a charity distributing menstrual products to girls and women in the UK, India, America and Nairobi, as well as teaching girls about menstruation. In India, they teach women to make their own pads.

> Freedom 4 Girls – charity striving to tackle period poverty distributing products in the UK, Uganda and Kenya.

> Irise International – global NGO working to find sustainable solutions to period poverty in the UK and East Africa.

> Hey Girls – social enterprise creating environmentally-friendly period products to address period poverty.

Audre Lorde:

'I AM NOT FREE WHILE ANY WOMAN IS UNFREE, EVEN WHEN HER SHACKLES ARE VERY DIFFERENT FROM MY OWN.'

4

GENDER PAY GAP

'The master's tools will never dismantle the
master's house.'

Audre Lorde

The gender pay gap is an element of patriarchy that it can be hard to galvanise interest around. Many of us, understandably, are more concerned with state violence, misogyny in the far right, violence against women and girls, and the repression of abortion rights; I know these things strike a chord more readily with me and invoke a more visceral reaction. Nevertheless, the gender pay gap is far more important than many assume. Since women entered the professional world of work around 100 years ago there has been great progress; however, we are still not being sufficiently compensated for our time and contribution, while many of our male counterparts are. It is a reality that sees men have more opportunities, liberties and success across the world, and women left in more unstable financial positions.

Analysing data from the Office for National Statistics, the Fawcett Society – the UK's leading gender equality charity – estimated that the mean hourly gender pay gap for full-time workers was currently 11.3 per cent, while it was 11.9 per cent in 2021, and 10.6 per cent in 2020.[58] The charity also issued a warning: it was 'deeply disappointing' that the gender pay gap in wider society has scarcely narrowed in recent years.

But what is driving the gender pay gap? It is a combination of many factors:

> Pay discrimination.

> Outrageously high childcare costs forcing women to curb their hours or retreat from the workplace altogether.

> Women being more likely to take on the burden of unpaid care for children or sick or elderly loved ones.

> The fact that women are radically overrepresented in low-paid, precarious forms of employment – many of which involve zero-hours contracts – such as healthcare, hospitality, admin, retail, cleaning and care work.

> The fact that women are underrepresented in the highest-paid types of work and less likely to be in the top jobs in a range of professions.

> The fact that women in the highest-paid jobs are often paid less than their male counterparts or even male colleagues in more junior positions.

Lamentably, many of these issues were compounded by austerity measures in the UK imposed by the coalition government and the Conservative Party since 2010, the Covid-19 pandemic of 2020 onwards and now again by the cost-of-living crisis. In a nutshell, it has been women who have been among those hardest hit by these consecutive crises. Nevertheless, it can be hard to drum up enduring interest in the gender pay gap. As many learn the hard way, too much of something is rarely a good thing, and the gamut of well-deserved headlines about the gender pay gap, coupled with the torpid progress on this problem, means you get the sense that people have switched off from the issue.

This is by no means to say the media coverage of the gender pay gap is scant. If anything, the opposite is true, though the press attention seems not to have been as impactful as many campaigners and politicians might have hoped. This could be because the gender pay gap is something that requires a bit of homework to properly understand, with misconceptions prevailing – an example being when the gender pay gap is blamed on the fallacy that women are simply less likely to broach the subject of asking for a pay rise. Research has found women ask for a pay rise just as often as men, but are less likely to receive one.[59] Of course, none of the aforementioned is helped by the Tories' lack of political urgency to invoke support for this issue or to tackle it.

The lack of drive to address the gender pay gap could also be linked to the dearth of women in leadership positions across a range of sectors. After all, men dominate a long list of areas of public life, with women woefully underrepresented in senior roles in politics, the NHS, finance, the law, trade unions, the civil service, the charitable sector, sports bodies and more. If we had more women in senior positions, perhaps more organisations would implement measures that tackle the gender pay gap. However, this is an optimistic view to take, which arguably places too much emphasis on the power of representation.

While getting more women into senior positions so our institutions better reflect wider society is important, it would be naive to assume that simply getting more women into positions of power will instantaneously turn the world into a utopia. Not all women want to tackle the gender pay gap, nor do all women want to create a less racist, less patriarchal and more equal society. You only have to look at the sentiments espoused by some of the most famous female politicians in the UK currently to see that this is the case.

Unsurprisingly, the gender pay gap is not uniform across the UK, with the chasm more extreme in certain parts of the country. What's more, the gender pay gap is worst for our oldest workers, while women workers from Black, Asian and minority ethnic backgrounds are paid less on average than white workers.[60] This is why the Labour Party, along with prominent campaigners, wants firms to be forced to publish their ethnicity pay gaps. The government rolled out rules forcing private companies and organisations who employ more than 250 people to release their gender pay gap figures in 2017, but the policy was temporarily suspended when the pandemic hit in 2020 as a result of the Covid chaos. MPs and charities repeatedly called for ministers to urgently reinstate gender pay gap reporting, but their demands were ignored.

So how does the UK compare to other countries who are tackling the gender pay gap? Is there more progress elsewhere? Research by King's College London and the Fawcett Society found that the UK takes a uniquely 'light-touch approach' to addressing the gender pay gap in the private sector and trails behind other nations.[61] In the UK, it has never been compulsory for private sector employers to produce an action plan to address pay bias. This massively differs from France where legislation means that if private sector workplaces do not get an adequate score across a set of gender pay gap barometers, an action plan must be drawn up with trade unions or employee reps.

Moreover, while in the UK a woman must go to a tribunal to discover what her male colleague earns if she fears she is being unfairly paid, in some parts of the world it is much easier to find out about co-workers' salaries. In Norway, for instance, everyone is able to learn how much another individual is paid by their employer because the information is freely available online. But looking beyond Europe, it is clear that unpaid labour augments gender pays gaps globally. Research by UNICEF suggests young women and girls taking on more household chores than boys plays a part in gender inequality around the world.

Back in the UK, it is important to note that girls have historically done better than boys in terms of GCSE results since the 1980s, with research finding, perhaps unsurprisingly, that girls do more homework. This trend surpasses GCSE level, though, with females doing better than their male counterparts throughout the education system. In fact, the gulf stretches from the early years to SATs, GCSEs, A-levels, university admittance and then to their grade of degree. Richard Adams, the *Guardian*'s education editor, notes that this is not the case just in the UK but 'in every developed country, with few exceptions'.[62]

However, when we move into the world of work, this trend is reversed, with men overtaking women in pay and today, we still see women underrepresented in senior roles across a vast range of sectors. Research from the end of 2022 found that a meagre 1 in 25 chief executives in Britain's biggest publicly listed firms was a woman.[63] This research, which looked at senior positions in the FTSE 350 largest companies listed on the London Stock Exchange, revealed that men make up a whopping 96 per cent of CEOs even though entry-level recruitment to the jobs is frequently nearly equal in terms of men and women employees.

Some will argue, or secretly think, this is because men

make better leaders than women. Whether we like it or not, the age-old notion that men are more suited to leadership is stubbornly ingrained – even though the data shows this is not the case. Research has shown that nations led by women fared better than average during the coronavirus crisis, and that firms in the top quartile for having more women in executive teams were 25 per cent more likely to have higher-than-average levels of profits than firms in the bottom quartile.[64] These are just some of the many reasons why we need women to be represented and fairly compensated across the board.

THE STATS

> Of over 1.6 million people in the UK who were not working due to caring for their family between February and April 2023, 85 per cent were women.[65]

> Studies have shown that women bore the brunt of childcare responsibilities, household chores and home-schooling during the Covid lockdowns, irrespective of whether they were working or not.

> The gender pay gap grows 'dramatically' wider after women have children, with the average working woman effectively spending almost two months of her year working for free in comparison to male counterparts.[66]

> NHS figures show that more than 80 per cent of adult social services jobs in 2019 were carried out by female workers, while government figures show that women make up the majority of informal carers in the UK.[67]

> Almost half a million women are classed as 'sandwich carers' in the UK, meaning they are caring for both children and

adult relatives – a higher number than men in the equivalent situation.[68]

> Girls spend 40 per cent more time doing household tasks than boys, which include getting water and firewood. Worldwide, this time girls spend on chores amounts to 160 million hours per day.[69]

> Progress on gender equality is moving at a 'glacial' speed, with research finding women are underrepresented in senior roles in a range of sectors.[70]

> Black women are the least likely section of society to be among the top earners in Britain.[71]

> Women were 96 per cent more likely than men to have been laid off due to the crisis caused by the pandemic.[72]

> In 2022 in the US, women earned an average of 82 per cent of what their male counterparts made.[73]

> The gender pay gap transcends borders, with estimates indicating that women earn an average of 16 per cent less than men around the world, but this gulf is far wider in many countries.[74]

> Women spend far more time than men doing three-quarters of the unpaid work around the world. Research has found that this amounts to 11 billion hours a day.[75]

THE WINS

> The Equal Pay Act, which was implemented in 1970, made equivalent pay for the same work a legal right more than half a century ago. Nevertheless, pay discrimination remains prevalent.

> Rules obliging companies and other organisations in the UK to release their respective gender pay gap figures were implemented in 2017.

> In 2022, the UK government announced that under new legislation employees would be given the right to ask for flexible working as soon as they start a job, with ministers saying they will 'make flexible working the default'.

> Labour promises it will force organisations with more than 250 employees to report their gender and ethnicity pay gaps, as well as provide action plans to address pay discrepancies, with outsourced workers included in this if they get into power.

RESOURCES

> Fawcett Society – leading gender equality charity campaigning on the gender pay gap.

> Young Women's Trust – charity helping young women aged 18 to 30 on low or no pay.

> IWGB, Unite and Unison – prominent trade unions.

> Close the Gap – Scottish organisation striving to tackle women's inequality in the workplace.

> Equal Pay Day – day which draws attention to the gender pay gap marked around the world.

5

MEN AND THE FAR RIGHT

'I imagine one of the reasons people cling to their hates so stubbornly is because they sense, once hate is gone, they will be forced to deal with pain.'

James Baldwin

In the same way that the far right is predominantly made up of men, the individuals who study the far right are also overwhelmingly male. This may partially explain why the misogynistic views that imbue far-right ideology often do not receive the attention they require. Nevertheless, awareness of the symbiotic relationship between the two schools of thought is thankfully growing. While I am not someone who buys into the ludicrous perspective that weed is a gateway drug for crack and heroin, it is a helpful analogy in this context. Misogyny (a hypothetical spliff) is often the gateway drug that lures men into more extreme and toxic far-right schools of thought, which can encourage violence and abuse, among other things.

Now, while the far-right spectrum is in no way a unified, monolithic global movement, misogyny and male supremacy are things that rear their ugly heads throughout the far right. In recent years, the far right has ballooned in size and power around the world, with the so-called alt-right, white supremacist movements, xenophobic populism, anti-migrant groups, the Identitarian movement and incels all falling under this same noxious banner. But far-right sentiment has not just swelled at the grassroots, activist levels; it has also found new and reinvigorated power in the political sphere. In the twenty-first century, far-right parties in Western Europe have become increasingly, disturbingly popular. This has spanned from the growing popularity of far-right populist parties in France, Spain, Germany, Sweden, Finland and Greece. After all, French far-right leader Marine Le Pen won a historic 13.3 million votes – which amounts to just over 41 per cent of the total – in April 2022. Moreover, authoritarian demagogues have also gained power at the national level, winning elections and becoming world leaders – as we have seen in Brazil, Italy, Hungary, Poland, Turkey, the Philippines and the US.

The far-right renaissance has been coupled with an acrimonious backlash against gender equality. A key example includes gender studies being banned in Hungary. When announcing the ban, Deputy Prime Minister Zsolt Semjén made the bigoted, flawed and nonsensical argument that gender studies 'has no business in universities' because it is 'an ideology, not a science' while a spokesperson for Viktor Orbán, Hungary's far-right prime minister – a world leader who has been called 'Trump before Trump' by Steve Bannon – said: 'The government's standpoint is that people are born either male or female, and we do not consider it acceptable for us to talk about socially constructed genders rather than biological sexes.' In 2019,

Orbán, who has earned the moniker of 'Viktator', announced Hungary will ensure mothers who have at least four children do not have to pay income tax for their entire lives in an attempt to drive up birth rates, as well as offering subsidies for families with more children to buy larger cars.

As you have probably already gathered, far-right thought often employs reductive, essentialist notions of biology, which favour nature over nurture, in a bid to bolster views of male dominance and supremacy over women and to transmute women into submissive breeding machines. This stretches back to the famous Nazi slogan '*Kinder, Küche, Kirche*', which was centred around Hitler's belief that women's lives should exist around children, cooking and church. Such views might sound antiquated to many, but the notion women should stay home to serve their male partner and look after the kids remains prevalent in the far right.

Another core element of current far-right attitudes to women involves weaponising violence against them to further racist, xenophobic ideals by pushing the idea white women must be protected against migrants. This repulsive phenomenon, which manifests in a range of ways, ran rampant during the 2015 so-called refugee crisis. Since then, these issues have become even more pressing as the so-called 'alt-right' movement – which has been widely associated with racism, antisemitism and misogyny – amassed growing power and attention in the wake of Trump's presidential bid and his time in Washington's corridors of power. Meanwhile, another key tenant of far-right thought often centres around a fierce animosity and disgust towards feminism. Take the crowds at rallies for the former far-right Brazilian president Jair Bolsonaro who chanted they would feed feminists dog food.

Research, entitled 'When Women Are the Enemy: The Intersection of Misogyny and White Supremacy', previously found that misogyny is a key element of the so-called alt-right movement. Researchers at the Anti-Defamation League discovered that the increasingly popular narrative of white men being victims of feminism has been a key driving force behind the misogyny that has become rife in far-right movements. The report argues that hatred of women is a 'dangerous and underestimated component of extremism'.[76] Of course, the far right is not only profoundly misogynistic, but also racist, homophobic, transphobic and xenophobic.

The incel movement would arguably be one of the most overt examples of the intersection between the far right and misogyny. An incel, which stands for a combination of the words 'involuntary' and 'celibate', is a heterosexual man who desperately wants to have sex with women but fails to do so, consequently heaping blame on women for his own inability to form sexual relationships. Jake Davison, a self-proclaimed incel, shot dead five people in the unlikely port city of Plymouth on the south coast of Devon – with his mother, Maxine, and a three-year-old girl among his victims – before aiming the gun at his own head on a sunny summer evening in August 2021. Davison, who had a track record of violence, was fixated on mass shootings, guns and serial killers.

After the tragedy, it emerged that Davison, who was diagnosed with autism in 2011, had previously uploaded videos referring to himself as an 'incel' and lamenting the fact that he had not lost his virginity as a teenager. Davison's murder spree was the deadliest mass shooting to take place in the UK in over a decade. This is just one tragic example of the deadly nature of the incel movement and sadly there are more. Incel men, who are affiliated with far-right, neo-Nazi movements, victimise themselves and attribute their dearth of sexual and romantic relationships to problems with society, construing women as the common nemesis. Incel communities, which have grown in recent years, have sprung up on Reddit, Facebook, 4chan and on websites established by incels themselves. Members of the dark community spout hate-filled, misogynistic abuse about women on online forums, as well as venting about people who are sexually active and making vitriolic comments about the women who reject them – even plotting against them.

Of course, hatred of women is not always this obvious among the far right. Take Andrew Tate, for instance. The former kick-boxing world champion turned self-avowed 'success coach', who is one of the most googled people in the world, claims 'women are the most precious things on the planet'.[77] Tate claims he loves women but simultaneously argues that men and women are unreservedly different. For this reason, he believes in very distinct gender roles, which remind me of a bygone era I am not keen to return to: the 1950s. Tate posits himself as an 'alpha male', as well as openly admitting he is a misogynist. Tate has argued it is 'disgusting' and 'revolting' for women to have lots of sexual partners but men are allowed to. Tate once referred to married women as 'property' that their husbands own, and I have previously reported on research by the Center for Countering Digital Hate, which unearthed 47 videos of Tate pushing what it describes as 'extreme misogyny'. The report uncovered adverts on videos where Tate discusses abusing women, encouraging his audience to 'grip her up by the neck' in one video, which has been viewed 1.6 million times, as well as referring to putting his 'imprint' on 18–19-year-old girls in other footage, which has accrued 8.4 million views.[78]

But who is Tate? His content on TikTok has been viewed more than 12.7 billion times at the time of writing. It is worth noting that nobody else on the popular video-sharing platform comes anywhere near this number. Whether you love him or hate him, Tate has accrued fame and 'success' at an extraor-dinary rate. And I would hazard a guess that it is this that his apostles hold so dear. They are drawn in by his opulent lifestyle, which centres around ostentatious cars, shiny private jets and upsettingly garish properties. People love Tate's inane video soliloquies, too, many of which I genuinely struggle to make sense of. They remind me of a certain caricature stoner at a house party trying to be incredibly deep and profound but who is making absolutely no sense and is spouting braindead, pointless gibberish.

Now, Tate, who has been banned from a number of social media platforms for hate speech and voicing misogynistic views, would not like being in this chapter as he does not market himself as being far right. And, to be fair, his nonsensical ramblings do subvert the traditional spectrum of left- and right-wing politics. But the extremity of Tate's misogynistic, homophobic, racist content does feel like it shares parallels with the far right, with experts warning that it can open the door to young men accessing material that is even more extreme.

In essence, the uncompromisingly hateful and cruel views of the far right can be difficult to make sense of. The comments I receive from online trolls, some of whom appear to be on the far right, not only are belligerent but often feel disconcertingly estranged from reality. Many trolls engage in 'whataboutism', defined by the Merriam-Webster Dictionary as 'the act or practice of responding to an accusation of wrongdoing by claiming that an offense committed by another is similar or worse'. If you have ever had a debate with someone and felt like they weren't properly listening to you and were completely missing the point of what you were saying, you may have encountered 'whataboutism' without knowing the name for it. When someone on Twitter wields 'whataboutism', it makes debating with them impossible and futile.

Not that I bother with that. Life is far too short.

THE STATS

> Men made up the overwhelming majority of the 2017 'Unite the Right' rally in Charlottesville in Virginia, which saw ugly clashes between neo-Nazis, KKK members and alt-right supporters and anti-fascists. A 32-year-old woman, Heather Heyer, was killed after a car ploughed into a group of anti-fascist protesters in a separate incident.

> A Secret Service report has found that men who label themselves 'involuntary celibates' are a growing threat in America, with researchers examining a slew of instances where men linked to incel movements have killed women.[79]

> Andrew Tate has substantial connections with the far right, which means the misogynistic influencer is a danger to young men and teenage boys, research by Hope not Hate warns.[80]

> Tate has stated that he has spent time with Tommy Robinson 'untold times', referring to the former English Defence League leader as being a 'solid guy' with a 'good heart'.[81]

> In elections stretching from 1988 to 1995 in Austria, France and Germany, the radical right's electorate was approximately 40 per cent women and 60 per cent men.[82]

RESOURCES

> Mapping the Global Far-Right – examines far-right groups.

> Hope Not Hate – leading charity campaigning against fascism and racism as well as working with schools to confront hate.

> Southern Poverty Law Center – monitors far-right and hate groups in the US and campaigns for racial justice.

> Small Steps – delivers anti-extremism training.

6

CHILDCARE

'There can be no keener revelation of a society's soul than the way in which it treats its children.'

Nelson Mandela

Given that we have free healthcare, free education and social security benefits in the UK, it always strikes me as strange that we do not have proper provision for childcare. Even though it's a resource that is integral to the running of a healthy, happy and prosperous economy, it doesn't get the attention it so desperately deserves. Moreover, while childcare constitutes a core part of the welfare states of some other nations, it has never been properly subsidised in the UK.

Britain's chronically underfunded childcare system is a massive driver of gender inequality. The cost of childcare just keeps rising. Data from the Organisation for Economic Co-operation and Development (OECD) demonstrates that the UK has either the world's most expensive childcare or the third most expensive – contingent on which way you look at the figures.[83] But either way, it is not pretty. Meanwhile, research by prominent campaign group Pregnant Then Screwed has found that around three in ten new parents will not be able to afford to have any more children, while almost half of pregnant mothers will have to shorten their maternity leave because of economic struggles.[84]

The charity has also discovered that six in ten women who have had an abortion say the cost of childcare in the UK put them off pregnancy, while almost one in five said childcare costs were the main reason they decided to terminate a pregnancy.[85] Having interviewed women who were forced to terminate wanted pregnancies because of fears of being unable to afford the child's care, I can tell you their stories were heartbreaking. These women did not consider their abortion as a choice made of their own volition; instead, it was a result of factors outside of their control.

Pregnant Then Screwed's research discovered that the situation was far starker for Black women, with three in four saying childcare costs were behind their decision to have an abortion, while the same proportion of single parents said the same. Childcare costs pushing women to have abortions must not be overlooked and should be considered when the government raises concerns that the UK birth rate is at a record low.

After all, unless you earn an astronomical salary, it often makes more financial sense to leave work and look after children than to pay the huge fees for childcare. Bleakly enough, other research by Pregnant Then Screwed found that for three-quarters of mothers who fork out for childcare, it doesn't make financial sense to carry on working.[86] Pregnant Then Screwed is campaigning for childcare to cost no more than 5 per cent of household income, a reasonable ask that I am sure many parents and non-parents can rally behind. Childcare currently constitutes 30 per cent of household income in the

UK, the organisation notes, but is an even higher percentage in London.[87]

It is fair to say that childcare isn't widely considered a glamorous, juicy or headline-grabbing topic, with this perhaps going some way to explaining why the issue has been historically excluded from top-level government decision-making. For me, the woeful neglect of childcare is a by-product of deeply entrenched misogyny and society's implicit assumption that women should stay at home and look after the kids. On top of this, the collective disregard for childcare is also linked to the wider dearth of attention and support given to mothers and children – a demographic of society often relegated to the so-called private sphere, where they are rendered invisible.

And yet high-quality, accessible, affordable childcare would greatly buoy the UK economy, as well as make the country more equal. We know that when it is done right, childcare curtails the attainment chasm between the most affluent children and those who walk the breadline. So, given that the consensus clearly states that the early years are a critical barometer for how a person will fare in later life, why do we not invest more in childcare?

It is not all doom and gloom, however. There has been significant progress in raising awareness of childcare in recent years. The hard work of campaigners has enabled the issue to ascend the political agenda. Childcare was the centrepiece of the 2023 spring budget, with Jeremy Hunt, chancellor of the Exchequer, announcing that the government would offer up to 30 hours of free childcare for children aged between nine months and their third birthday for parents working more than 16 hours in England. While the new policy has been welcomed with a heavy sigh of relief, the policy has also come under fire, because it will not come into full force until autumn 2025. Campaigners and childcare providers themselves have also raised fears that the money promised to deliver the policy is wholly inadequate and fails to tackle the crisis engulfing nurseries and early-years providers.

The childcare sector is already battling a funding deficit and issues with staff retention, with employees leaving in droves – often citing feeling underpaid, undervalued and overworked. Some 20,000 early-years providers in England shut their doors between March 2015 and March 2022.[88] Across the Atlantic, the childcare sector is also in crisis mode, with parents finding childcare highly expensive and those who work in the sector being tremendously underpaid. It is often mothers who are hardest hit, as they are more likely to take on the burden of childcare and see their careers suffer as a result. If childcare were properly subsidised, we might even see women higher up in workforces, perhaps shrinking the gender pay gap.

It need not be this way; you only have to look at Scandinavian countries, where parents receive support during pregnancy and beyond, to see that high-quality and affordable childcare can be a reality. Even though, in the UK, there is more attention than ever before on the damaging repercussions the extortionate cost of childcare has on society as a whole, far more conversations need to be had.

THE STATS

> The UK's paternity benefit ranks as the worst in Europe, with the number of fathers taking paternity leave plummeting to a 10-year low in 2020/21, with only around a quarter of eligible fathers taking time off work after their child is born.[89]

> One study has found that childcare costs are higher than the rent or mortgage for a third of parents using childcare, as well as 38 per cent of single parents and 47 per cent of Black parents.[90]

> There were 2.5 million families with a lone mother in the UK as of 2022 – with women making up 84 per cent of single parents.[91]

> The average cost of a full-time nursery place for a toddler under the age of two in the UK is £14,836 per year, research has found.[92]

> Less than one in five local authorities in England say they have sufficient childcare places for disabled children – a decrease from previous years.[93]

> Childcare costs have massively increased in the UK since 2015, while wage growth has slowed down.[94]

> Around 54,000 mothers are estimated to be driven out of the workforce every year in cases of pregnancy discrimination.[95]

> Three-quarters of mothers who spend money on childcare report that working has stopped making sense in terms of their finances.[96]

> Around half of people in the US live in a 'childcare desert' – with the country's childcare crisis for infant toddlers costing $122 billion annually.[97]

THE WINS

> In the 1970s, Scandinavian countries became the first in the world to provide families with childcare funded by the state.

> All new mothers have been receiving Finland's Maternity Package, which is widely known as a 'baby box', since the 1930s – the box contains 64 items in total, including a book and clothes, and the scheme has been mirrored in other countries around the world.

> New Labour launched flagship Sure Start centres in 1998 in a bid to help children in low-income families, with 3,600 centres in operation at the project's zenith in 2010, but local authority spending cuts have seen many centres close in recent years.

> The government introduced 30 hours of free childcare per week in term time for three- and four-year-olds in England in 2017, although research exposed that the government deliberately underfunded the scheme by nearly £3 per child for every hour.

> In September 2022, Labour unveiled plans if elected for wholly funded breakfast clubs for all primary schools in England.[98]

> Over 15,000 families were estimated to have marched in cities up and down the UK for a Halloween-themed protest entitled March of the Mummies in October 2022, calling for the government to urgently solve the childcare crisis and improve maternity and paternity provision.

> In spring 2023, Labour pledged to overhaul the current childcare system if it wins the next election, committing to delivering support from the point at which parental leave ends until the age of 11.

> The UK government announced 30 hours of free childcare for all under-fives from the point at which maternity care ends for working parents in the 2023 Spring Budget.

RESOURCES

> Pregnant Then Screwed – prominent campaign group fighting to tackle extortionate childcare costs and lack of support for pregnant women and mothers.

> Gingerbread – leading single-parent charity.

> Working Families – helping working parents and carers as well as aiming to eradicate workplace obstacles for those with caring responsibilities.

> Early Years Alliance – represents nurseries, pre-schools and registered childminders.

7

POLICING

'If one really wishes to know how justice is administered in a country, one does not question the policemen, the lawyers, the judges, or the protected members of the middle class. One goes to the unprotected – those, precisely, who need the law's protection most! – and listens to their testimony.'

James Baldwin

Can you think of a more universally hated institution in the world than the police? I don't know about you, but I am hard-pressed to think of one. Many issues with policing transcend countries' borders, and this is reflected in the fact that you will find the four letters ACAB – which stand for All Cops Are Bastards – spray-painted on walls around the world. Condemnation and distrust of the police pervade both communities and popular culture. After all, there is no other arm of the state that has been christened with so many slang descriptions.

While distrust and contempt towards the police are caused by an abundance of factors, a great deal of animosity is fuelled by certain officers abusing the immense power they have at their disposal. In many ways, the police hold more power than any other component of the state. Yes, a judge can confine you to life in prison, and social services can remove your kids from your care, but there is no other institution that routinely employs brute physical force against citizens of its own country. Yes, the armed forces do so in some countries, but the police do this on a global scale.

Bear in mind that at least 1,238 people are estimated to have been killed by the police in the US in 2022.[99] This was the deadliest year of police violence since records started in 2013, with an average of more than three people killed by the police per day. Mapping Police Violence, which documents those killed by police since 2013, states Black people are almost three times more likely to be killed by police than white people in America. The lives claimed include people fatally shot, tasered, beaten or restrained to death. The organisation states every year, less than three per cent of killings by police lead to officers being charged with a crime. 'Our analysis suggests a substantial proportion of all killings by police in 2022 could have been prevented and that specific policies and practices might prevent police killings in the future,' the organisation says in its 2022 Police Violence Report.[100]

Of course, there are other facets of the police's far-reaching power. After all, there is no other part of the state that can legally, legitimately enter and search the space most of us hold dearest: our home. Police can not only get a warrant to rifle through your most personal possessions in a raid; they can also make life in your local community hell if they so wish, harassing you via incessantly stopping and searching you.

While men more often bear the brunt of police brutality, police violence also impacts on women. Given the remit of this book, this will be my focus. Police-perpetrated domestic abuse and sexual violence against women in the UK is an issue I have written about a fair amount, having interviewed women who accuse the police of abhorrent domestic abuse and sexual violence – these women were in relationships with officers, married to them or members of the public.

Thankfully, and rightly, this is an issue that has gained increasing awareness since Sarah Everard was murdered by a serving Metropolitan Police officer in March 2021. Wayne Couzens, a firearms officer at Britain's largest police force, wielded coronavirus lockdown restrictions to falsely arrest Everard, a 33-year-old marketing executive, before kidnapping, raping, strangling and murdering her. Couzens was sentenced to a whole-life prison term and will die in jail. It has since emerged that the police missed opportunities to pinpoint Couzens as a sex offender.

Couzens is said to have been nicknamed 'the rapist' by colleagues because he made female officers feel uncomfortable, and was also accused of several instances of indecent exposure going back to 2015 – legally defined as deliberately displaying your genitals in a public space to trigger alarm or distress – before killing Everard. Couzens pleaded guilty to committing indecent exposure in 2023, admitting to exposing his genitals in three incidents in November 2020 and February 2021.

Since then, the Met Police and other police forces across the UK have been engulfed by a spate of scandals involving violence against women. Time and time again, it has been asked how an institution that fails to tackle abuse against women perpetrated within its own ranks can be trusted to deal with these issues in the wider community.

Take the jaw-dropping 363-page Casey Review, commissioned in the wake of Everard's murder and released in March 2023, which reached the conclusion that the Met Police is institutionally racist, misogynist and homophobic.[101] The report discovered that a 'culture of denial' had allowed predators to flourish, and officers had used their position of power for sexual purposes. A shocking litany of horrors was unearthed by the report, including but not limited to: Black Londoners disproportionately being subjected to stop and search, Black officers being 81 per cent more likely to face disciplinary action, and female officers facing sexual assault and harassment from officers. The review also revealed that an aspiring special constable who had a juvenile conviction for indecent exposure, which involved him exposing himself to the same woman a whopping seven times by masturbating at his bedroom window after trying to get her attention by coughing, was allowed to join after managing to appeal against previous rejections.

The report bolsters Baroness Louise Casey's previous review into the Met Police, which revealed that hundreds of officers should have been fired for serious misconduct and breaching the law – exposing the force's inability to get rid of officers accused of sexual assault, domestic abuse and discrimination. The initial Casey Review, released in October 2022, found that less than 1 per cent of officers with multiple allegations against them had been let go by the Met Police.[102] 'Based on this report, which clearly says that we have been far too soft, there must be hundreds in the organisation I need to get rid of,' Met Police chief Sir Mark Rowley said in the wake of the review. 'Some of them are unethical and don't deserve to be a cop and don't deserve to wear the uniform. And some of what they're doing is in many cases criminal.'

It is fast emerging that the police systems that decide who can become an officer are often not fit for purpose. Cressida

Dick, former Met Police chief, completely missed the mark when she said there is an occasional 'bad 'un' in Britain's largest police force. While it wasn't a credible comment at the time, it has aged even more badly, now appearing darkly comical. Problems with policing are not confined to bad apples; they are rooted in an institution that is rotten to the core. Yes, there are people who join the police for the right reasons, but this ceases to eradicate the legacies and cultures of unspeakable injustice, discrimination and brutality that permeate policing.

Of course, in the US, police violence takes on a different meaning, as officers are armed with guns and are more militarised than UK police. What's more, in America, the history of the police cannot be extricated from the history of slavery, with slave patrols forming the genesis of US policing. Set up to catch enslaved people who ran away from their masters in the South, slave patrols captured 'fugitives' and returned them to their masters. While slavery in the US may have been abolished in 1865 and segregation laws in 1964, the current war on drugs, the billions of pounds pumped into US policing and the huge profits reaped from the so-called 'prison industrial complex', all of which disproportionately impact people of colour, mean things have not changed anywhere near as much in the US as is sometimes touted.

For those wondering what the prison industrial complex is, Merriam-Webster Dictionary describes it as 'the profit-driven relationship between the government, the private companies that build, manage, supply, and service prisons, and related groups (such as prison industry unions and lobbyists) regarded as the cause of increased incarceration rates especially of poor people and minorities and often for non-violent crimes'. In layman's terms, it means the government and big companies profit from more prisoners, and so the rate of imprisonment is higher. It is no surprise that in America, a country that is home to a large chunk of the world's prison population, you most often hear this term and see it play out in reality.

But let's return to the issue of policing in the UK. It is impossible to understand police failures without scrutinising the cultures in which they operate. Sue Fish, a former police chief I interviewed for *The Independent*, told me police officers routinely perpetrate 'appalling bullying and blanking' when officers accuse colleagues of sexism and sexual offences.[103] The former Nottingham Police chief told me many police officers' entire social lives revolve around hanging out with other officers and many meet partners through policing. Fish warned of a 'laddy culture' in policing which means misogyny and sexual advances are tolerated. To sum up, the deeply ingrained institutional issues that afflict policing sadly appear to show no sign of retreating, but at least there is growing awareness of these problems.

THE STATS

> The landmark 1999 Stephen Lawrence Inquiry concluded that the Metropolitan Police was institutionally racist, finding that the investigation into the killing of Stephen Lawrence was 'marred by a combination of professional incompetence, institutional racism and a failure of leadership'.[104]

> Police officers are enabled to abuse their partners with impunity by a 'locker room culture', which turns a blind eye to domestic abuse, Centre for Women's Justice research has found.[105]

> Hundreds if not thousands of police officers who should have failed vetting checks may be in the job in England and

Wales, with a watchdog discovering many cases where individuals should not have been permitted to become police officers, even including predatory sex offenders and those with organised crime connections.[106]

> Research by Inquest has found that Black people are seven times more likely to die than white people in the wake of the police wielding restraint.[107]

> Met Police officers were criticised for aggressively grabbing women who were paying tribute to Sarah Everard at a peaceful vigil in Clapham, South London, in March 2021 before taking them away while others screamed and cried out.

> The Met Police's budget has been slashed by 18 per cent in real terms since 2010, leading Britain's largest police force to axe two-thirds of its special constables and close 126 police stations.[108]

> Almost half of Black and minority ethnic domestic abuse survivors say police have failed to take their complaints seriously.[109]

> Some 16 per cent of deaths in police custody or in the wake of contact with the police since 1990 are individuals with Black, Asian and minoritised ethnicities, Inquest research has found.[110]

> Black children in England and Wales were up to six times more likely to be made to go through a pre-arrest strip-search, a report by the Children's Commissioner has found.[111]

RESOURCES

> Centre for Women's Justice – legal charity which tackles violence against women and focuses on police injustice.

> Reclaim These Streets – leading campaign group which focuses on policing, neighbourhood safety and protest rights.

> Network for Police Monitoring – coalition keeping tabs on and challenging police brutality and injustice.

> Stop Watch – Striving for policing to be fairer, as well as more just and accountable.

> Liberty – biggest civil liberties organisation in the UK.

> Inquest – UK's only organisation helping families whose loved one died after police contact, while imprisoned or in the care of mental health services.

> Mothers against Police Brutality – US organisation joining mothers to unite against police injustice and deadly force, as well as bringing together mothers whose children have died as a result of police brutality.

8

WOMEN'S HEALTH

'I'm interested in women's health because I'm a
woman. I'd be a darn fool not to be on my own side.'

Maya Angelou

The mind and the body are inextricably linked. This is not a
'conspirituality' theory, but rather a universally accepted fact
within medical discourse. Studies have found that chronic
pain and mental health issues can compound each other, with
those living with chronic pain more likely to struggle to sleep
and experience mental health issues, such as anxiety, depression and addiction.[112] And as hard as being in pain is, having
a health professional refute and downplay the agony you are
in makes the ordeal far more exasperating. Sadly, this is a situation far too many women find themselves in due to the gender
health gap – an issue that interlocks with other inequalities,
with racial health disparities also being a major issue.

Many women in the UK say they do not feel properly
listened to when accessing healthcare – feeling instead that

their issues go ignored or dismissed. Meanwhile, there are several studies that show how women's pain is often taken far less seriously than that of men.[113] This is likely to be a combination of misogyny and systemic top-down NHS issues, meaning health professionals are burnt out and overworked and sometimes have insufficient time to properly tend to their patients. This misogyny may often not be conscious or intentional, but its repercussions remain damaging. What's more, the data demonstrates that women are not only forced to spend longer stretches of time waiting in emergency departments; they are also less likely to be prescribed effective painkillers than men.[114] There are countless other examples of how scientific research has long overlooked women's bodies, with many of the conditions that only affect women receiving less funding for research.[115]

In a welcome rebalancing of the scales, and in an explicit bid to rectify 'decades of gender health inequality', the government launched its first ever Women's Health Strategy for England in July 2022, after almost 100,000 responses to a call for evidence. Researchers found that more than eight in ten women feel like health professionals do not listen to them – with the 127-page document rightfully stating 'historically, the health and care system has been designed by men, for men'.[116] The consultation also unveiled a health chasm between women in the most affluent parts of the country and those in the most impoverished areas. The consultation heard from thousands of women who said they 'persistently needed to advocate for themselves' and could not get a diagnosis without pressing for the issue to be looked at again.

The strategy came in the wake of the Cumberlege Review, published in 2020, which revealed that avoidable harm had been inflicted on tens of thousands of women and babies, with serious health issues downplayed as 'women's problems'.[117]

However, inadequate recording of data means the exact scale of the problem will never be disclosed. The major inquiry looked at everything from the use of vaginal mesh to the hormone pregnancy test Primodos, to an anti-epilepsy medicine called sodium valproate, which harmed unborn babies. It shed light on a troubling spate of healthcare scandals stretching over several decades. The inquiry, which was ordered by the government, heard how women often saw their symptoms unfairly blamed on psychological issues or it being 'that time of life', with 'anything and everything women suffer perceived as a natural precursor to, a part of, or a post-symptomatic phase of, the menopause'.[118] This is all the more painfully ironic when you consider that women who are actually suffering menopausal symptoms often see their struggles disregarded and overlooked by doctors.

Meanwhile, the poor women who had vaginal mesh surgery told those who conducted the review that they endured 'excruciating chronic pain … like razors inside their body, damage to organs, the loss of mobility and sex life and depression and suicidal thoughts'.[119] And these are by no means the only scandals that have predominantly impacted women.

Let's not forget rogue breast surgeon Ian Paterson, who was convicted of 17 counts of wounding with intent and three counts of unlawful wounding back in 2017. Paterson conducted unnecessary operations in NHS and private hospitals on more than 1,000 patients over the course of 14 years, an independent inquiry discovered, fabricating or overstating cancer risks and requesting payments for more pricey procedures. Paterson wasn't the only example of entrenched bias and misogyny in the health systems, however. Take the tragic avoidable deaths of more than 200 babies at the Shrewsbury and Telford Hospital NHS Trust, which constitutes the biggest maternity scandal in the history of the NHS. An inquiry into the scandal found that failings also resulted in hundreds of babies being stillborn, dying rapidly after they were born or being left with acute brain damage.[120]

Even among women themselves disparities thrive. Terrifying research published by MBRRACE-UK in November 2022 discovered that Black women are almost four times more likely to die from childbirth than white women.[121] The study also found that maternal death rates in deprived areas are rising, with women living in the most impoverished parts of the country being 2.5 times more likely to die than those in the least deprived areas.[122] Deep-rooted, knee-jerk misogyny means women's health issues are sometimes seen as trivial and tiresome, but all the above examples show that an inability to take them seriously can be highly dangerous. Yet still misinformation about women's health remains common. It is widely seen as normal to have painful periods, but often this can be an indication of another underlying health issue. As a result, chronic diseases such as endometriosis go undiagnosed and women struggle with symptoms for years without understanding the reason behind them. Moreover, research has shown that period pain can be as 'bad as having a heart attack' but period cramps are still routinely downplayed and sometimes even belittled.[123]

Medical inequity can also be seen in how many women are missed for diagnoses of ADHD and autism. A story I wrote revealed that tens of thousands more women tested themselves for autism in 2021, with the numbers seeking tests now far outstripping men.[124] Health professionals told me that the increase is a consequence of women not being diagnosed with neurodevelopmental disorders as children and teens due to autism wrongly being viewed as a male disorder. Meanwhile, experts said autistic women and girls are routinely overlooked and neglected by health services due to them being more likely to conceal or internalise symptoms. Similarly, with ADHD, all the traditional expectations of this form of neurodivergence are shaped around how it appears in men. Women display symptoms differently and are also more likely to mask them if they prove difficult in day-to-day life.

Many of these issues transcend the UK's borders – the World Health Organization has warned that the 'health of women and girls is of particular concern because, in many societies, they are disadvantaged by discrimination rooted in socio-cultural factors'. The organisation notes that 'women and girls face increased vulnerability to HIV/AIDS' and draws up a list of some 'socio-cultural factors' that block women from getting adequate healthcare. This includes: 'Unequal power relationships between men and women; social norms that decrease education and paid employment opportunities; an exclusive focus on women's reproductive roles; and potential or actual experience of physical, sexual and emotional violence.'[125]

The history and enduring legacy of gender and racial disparities in healthcare remain firmly entrenched and will take a long time to root out and reconfigure. However, on the bright side, at least there is greater discussion and subsequent awareness of these problems, and many women in the world of health and beyond are fiercely fighting to make change.

THE STATS

> LGBTQ+ women living in Britain are subjected to discrimination and prejudice when accessing healthcare services.[126]

> Endometriosis impacts around 1 in 10 women and girls who are of reproductive age, amounting to nearly 190 million women around the world.

> It takes an average of eight years for a woman in the UK to get an endometriosis diagnosis.[127]

> Around 13 babies die before, during or soon after birth each day in the UK.

> The number of pregnant and breastfeeding teenage girls and women experiencing acute malnutrition has risen by 25 per cent from 5.5 million to 6.9 million since 2020 in the 12 nations worst impacted by the global food and nutrition crisis.[128]

> Gynaecological health is one of the most under-prioritised areas of health around the world.[129]

> Women in low-income households in the UK are less likely to receive the healthcare they need and are more likely to stop work due to chronic pain.[130]

> A third of those with a women's health condition are made to wait three years or longer for a diagnosis in the UK, with almost three million women estimated to be grappling with symptoms of undiagnosed conditions.[131]

RESOURCES

> Wellbeing of Women – charity focusing on women's reproductive and gynaecological health.

> Royal College of Obstetricians and Gynaecologists – organisation that boosts women's healthcare around the world with over 16,000 members.

> Endometriosis UK – delivers support and resources for those impacted by endometriosis.

> Sands – organisation supporting those impacted by the death of a baby, before, during or just after birth.

> Médecins sans frontières – global organisation whose name means Doctors without Borders that delivers healthcare to individuals impacted by war and humanitarian crises.

9

CRIMINAL JUSTICE SYSTEM

'Mass imprisonment generates profits as it devours social wealth, and thus it tends to reproduce the very conditions that lead people to prison.'

Angela Davis

What comes to mind when you think of violence? Not psychological or material violence but brute force. I'd hazard a guess that when most people think of violence, they think of violence in the streets: a booze-fuelled late-night scrap between two men in a pub. Or knife or gun crime. But for women, it's more likely for serious violence to happen in the home.[132] And as we recall from Chapter 2, between two and three women are killed each week by their partners or ex-partners in England and Wales, showing that violence can happen very close to home indeed.

But there is another kind of violence that is far less widely talked about, and that is the violence perpetrated by the criminal justice system. In other words, the police, the courts and the prison system. It isn't hard to feel deeply cynical and disturbed by the UK's prison system and its inability to rehabilitate, or to feel distrustful of policing when forces are afflicted by consecutive scandals. While the chapters on Prisons (Chapter 15) and Policing (Chapter 7) will look at these issues in more depth, this chapter takes a broader look at what happens when women are drawn into the criminal justice system as purported or proven offenders rather than victims.

It is worth noting that many of these women have experienced violence, coercion, exploitation or mental health problems. Or they may be ensnared in the justice system because of the actions taken by their husband or partner, which they may have had very little control over or stake in. Of course, some of these relationships will be abusive and controlling, adding an additional layer of complexity to the situation. It is this wider understanding that is needed, because, although some women will have inarguably done wrong, many are victims of circumstance and have been let down by other systems way before they offended.

Joint enterprise laws – which sound far more innocuous than they are and should garner far more attention than they do – have pulled women into the criminal justice system time and time again, despite not being themselves involved in the alleged offence. The laws effectively enable numerous people to be convicted for one offence.

These laws have a starkly damaging impact on men, too, but that is for another book. Research released in 2020 found that joint enterprise laws were leading to women being jailed for life for violent crimes they did not commit.[133] The first-of-its-kind study conducted by Manchester Metropolitan University, which I reported on, unearthed new evidence revealing that at least 109 women have been sentenced to long prison sentences, including life sentences, under the joint enterprise system. Despite the fact that a 2016 Supreme Court ruling reached the conclusion that the law had 'taken a wrong turn' when it came to joint enterprise, the legal principle, which first emerged as far back as the Victorian era, continues to be used.

Meanwhile, MPs have previously warned that thousands of women are needlessly arrested and detained in custody each year before being released without charge. A report by the All-Party Parliamentary Group (APPG) on Women in the Penal System said this includes cases where women were in reality the victim of a crime, or were arrested while visibly distressed and when there have been fears about their mental health.[134] Also, many of these pointless arrests have been linked to incidents in the home where women have sought to defend themselves after being subjected to violence or abuse.

But what happens to those women who do wind up with a criminal record? Research has found that women are almost twice as likely as men to have their criminal records disclosed when applying for a job, as female-dominated sectors like care work and education entail more checks.[135] All of the aforementioned issues are far starker and more dramatic for women from Black and minoritised backgrounds. Data shows that minority ethnic women were two times more likely to be arrested than white women, while Black women were around 25 per cent more likely to be handed a custodial sentence at crown court than white women.[136]

At its core, the criminal justice system is routinely failing women and re-traumatising them. The government is very good at paying lip service to things that need to change but not following through with tangible action. Back in 2007, the Corston Report demanded a major overhaul of how the criminal justice system approaches women, with Baroness Corston calling for more women's centres to be rolled out and

'THE FUNCTION OF FREEDOM IS TO FREE SOMEONE ELSE.'

TONI MORRISON

for jail sentences to only be given for those violent offenders who could endanger others.[137] Sadly, many of the grave harms unearthed in this major report still wreak havoc on the lives of women and their families today.

After all, when you send anyone to prison, it has repercussions for their loved ones, especially the children of prisoners. As many as 17,000 children are estimated to be impacted by mothers being jailed every single year in England and Wales, with 95 per cent forced to pack up and leave their home when their mother is imprisoned.[138] A prisoner's problems often do not end when they hop, skip and jump out of the prison gates – as reoffending rates and housing issues for prisoners exemplify. Let's not forget that just 47 per cent of women departed prison with settled accommodation in the year ending in March 2022.[139]

The government's 2018 Female Offender Strategy set out the goal of having fewer women in jail, but MPs declared they had made scant developments in generating different options to prison. Moreover, given recent government forecasts saying the number of women in prison could substantially increase in the coming years, it feels neither defeatist nor hyperbolic to predict that the injustice of the criminal justice system will worsen.

It does not take a sociology professor to decipher that more often than not crime is caused by a lethal cocktail of chronic underinvestment of public services, lack of affordable housing, poverty, addiction, mental health problems, interpersonal violence and abuse, racial injustice, state violence and, ultimately, the upholding of patriarchy. As such, crime cannot be solved by simply cramming more people into prison. We must address these issues at their root, rather than just sticking our fingers in our ears, shouting 'la la la' and hoping for the best.

THE STATS

> Around eight in ten of those who came into contact with the criminal justice system in 2021 were men, while women made up around two in ten.[140]

> Men made up 85 per cent of arrests in 2021/22.[141]

> Almost 100,000 arrests of women are made in England and Wales every year, with 37,000 estimated to lead to no charges being pressed. Many of these needless arrests are linked to incidents in the home where women have sought to defend themselves after being subjected to violence or abuse.[142]

> Some 14 per cent of all women defendants at court were prosecuted for more serious offences, which take place in the Crown Court and generally necessitate a jury – this is substantially lower than the 23 per cent of male defendants prosecuted for such offences.[143]

> In a report carried out in 2020, MPs and peers drew attention to a case where a woman outside of a supermarket was arrested for begging, while another woman was arrested after stepping out into a main road continuously.[144]

> In the same report, Black, Asian and ethnic minority women were found to be more than twice as likely to be arrested as white women, yet less likely to be charged after their arrest.

> The Ministry of Justice estimates that the female prison population will have reached 4,300 by July 2025, which signifies a surge of 34 per cent more than the current population.[145]

❭ Brain injuries suffered at the hands of a violent partner could be leading women prisoners to commit more crimes, with research released in 2019 finding that two-thirds of female prisoners who have a brain injury say it was inflicted by an abusive partner.[146]

RESOURCES

❭ Revolving Doors – a charity which helps people trapped in a cycle of homelessness, crime and mental health issues.

❭ Transform Justice – a charity striving for a fair and compassionate justice system.

❭ Advance – working with women in the criminal justice system to disrupt cycles of offending.

❭ Criminal Justice Alliance – a network of more than 200 members striving towards a fair criminal justice system.

❭ Centre for Crime & Justice Studies – confronts criminal justice policies and works towards a less punitive justice system less centred around criminalisation.

❭ Clinks – a network helping the voluntary sector which operates in the criminal justice system.

10

WOMEN'S SEXUAL PLEASURE

'Love is never any better than the lover.'

Toni Morrison

Sex, drugs, rock 'n' roll: three entities perennially heralded as among life's greatest pleasures. However, of the three, it is sex that unequivocally has the most widespread appeal. For many, sex is one of the cardinal joys of being alive. This is why it strikes me as strange there is not more discussion about the orgasm gap between men and women. While there are burgeoning conversations, most are relatively recent and are often confined to the occasional column and discussions between sex thera-pists. Among society at large, there is surprisingly little interest or consternation in the gendered gulf in sexual pleasure, which, for the record, has one clear loser: heterosexual women.

In the UK, this is likely to be a reflection of the prudish and utilitarian approach we often take to sex. Intercourse is often portrayed as a means to an end – i.e. procreation – rather than celebrated as a source of pure, unbridled joy. Unless you are watching porn or at a sex-positive panel event or reading a women's mag, discussions of foreplay, masturbation and different sexual positions are rarely referenced. Everyone deserves to find pleasure in sex, and so I was happy to see a vibrator on display in a pharmacy in a small, non-touristy fishing village in Gran Canaria while on holiday last year; this is definitely not something you would encounter in a village in the UK.

To be clear, research has unwaveringly discovered that men have more orgasms than women. Take a report which analysed data from more than 50,000 Americans which found that lesbians orgasmed 86 per cent of the time while having sex, whereas straight women orgasmed 65 per cent of the time, while, surprise surprise, straight men came out on top, orgasming 95 per cent, substantially more than gay men who orgasmed 89 per cent of the time.[147]

But what is causing this orgasm gap? The blame cannot solely be heaped on uninspiring, lacklustre male lovers (although unfortunately there do appear to be a few of those around). Instead, the prevalence of the issue indicates systemic issues, which transcend the bedroom – a problem that stems, I would argue, from the historic taboo that surrounds female sexuality. Despite the fact that it is monopolised and neatly packaged to sell everything from cars to perfume to new television shows, when it comes down to it women's sexuality remains shrouded behind mystery and shame.

Historically, the dearth of knowledge and discussion of female sexuality means women have often been forced to endure an almost collective disassociation from their sexual desires and proclivities. This may have something to do with how historical amnesia has effectively erased the clitoris from existence. Scroll through medical textbooks and you will undoubtedly find diagrams of the penis, but the clitoris is rarely referred to.[148] Unsurprising when you learn that the first anatomical study of the clitoris was published in 1998.

What's more, the fact that we routinely use the wrong word for the vagina is arguably reflective of how history, science and society has effectively desexualised female genitalia. Instead of vagina, we should really be using the word vulva, which describes the entirety of the female sex organ, including the clitoris, urethral opening, labia and vagina. The vagina solely describes the canal that leads to the cervix. It seems pertinent and telling that the part of female genitalia we understand most fully and use as a reference is the part that the penis is inserted into and that gives birth to children. Throughout history women have been perceived via the male gaze and male understanding, and so omission and misunderstanding of women's bodies is rife even today. It is no secret that the penis is much more firmly entrenched in public consciousness and popular culture than the vulva is.

It is ironic that female pleasure is diminished and overlooked, because when sex is good, there is actually a reverse orgasm gap and it is the woman who is able to have far more orgasms in a heady, impassioned night of sex. Yet it is upsetting to think that there are swathes of women across the world who have never, ever reached climax – while having sex with another or masturbating. Nancy Stokes, a character played by veteran British actor Emma Thompson in the 2022 film *Good Luck to You, Leo Grande*, is a fictional example of this phenomenon. Stokes, a widowed and retired teacher in her fifties, hires a young, handsome male escort in a bid to finally experience her first orgasm.

Of course, women's sexuality is not just cloaked in taboos; it is seen as unsettling and intimidating by some. The continued prevalence of slut-shaming – something espoused by both men and women – is proof of how women's desire can be demonised and repressed. Slut-shaming appears to be the most acceptable form of misogyny in modern times. It comes from an age-old perception that a woman should be chaste or pure until she makes a long-term commitment to one person.

Many of the most vocal slut-shamers are men who have one rule for themselves and their male friends and a wholly different one for the women in their lives. Bogus, biologically deterministic misconceptions plague notions of sexuality. It is often thought that men have much higher sex drives than women – something which has little empirical basis but is routinely touted as a fact. Sexual attitudes are rife with gendered double standards. A man sleeps around and he is a player and a sex god; a woman does the same and she is a slag, a whore or a slut. In fact, there are hardly any derogatory words to describe a promiscuous man, though there are a wealth of them to describe promiscuous women.

The madonna–whore complex, a sentiment I believe many subscribe to, even if they have never heard of it, can go some way in explaining this. It is a famous psychoanalytic concept that was the brainchild of a man who will need no introduction to many: Sigmund Freud. The premise was ultimately an attempt by the neurologist who has been billed as the 'father of psychoanalysis' to explain men who cannot reconcile love and desire for their female partner. The concept seeks to explain those heterosexual men who divide women partners into the categories of madonna and whore. The madonna being cast as chaste, virtuous and pure, and the whore being cast as promiscuous, deviant and untrustworthy. In Freud's own words: 'Where such men love, they have no desire, and where they desire they cannot love'. The concept may explain the feeling many women have of being caught between a rock and a hard place, where if you are too sexually confident you are branded a slut and if you are too shy, you are dismissed as a dull prude.

Another element of sexuality that is beset by hypocrisy is masturbation. Jokes and throwaway comments about men wanking permeate popular culture, whereas the idea of a woman pleasuring herself continues to be a dirty little secret. The awkwardness I felt when I arrived at a hotel in Brighton and my vibrator started loudly, spontaneously gyrating in my suitcase as I greeted the receptionist, as well as my perpetual worry that it will be on view in a work Zoom call are perfect examples of the embarrassment and shame attached to masturbation for women. Saying that, women are now buying more sex toys than ever before, and we are seeing an increase of women directors in the porn industry. I hope we are heading towards a moment when female masturbation is accepted rather than stigmatised.

While we still have a long way to go until we're rid of gendered sexual inequalities, there has, however, been a good deal of progress on this issue – with more open and honest public dialogues about sex and desire.

THE STATS

> Homosexuality was classed as a mental illness by the American Psychiatric Association until 1973.

> When having sex, 80 per cent of heterosexual women feign orgasm around half of the time, while a quarter nearly always pretend they are orgasming.[149]

> There are twice as many nerve endings in the clitoris as in the penis – a clitoris is estimated to have 8,000, while a penis has 4,000.

> Polling of more than 50,000 Americans discovered that lesbians orgasmed 86 per cent of the time while having sex,

in comparison to straight women who orgasmed 65 per cent of the time. The figure was 95 per cent for straight men.[150]

> The UK is among the top four nations for accepting casual sex. The portion of people across all UK generations who deem casual sex as defensible has at least doubled since 2009.[151]

> While almost half of Australians consider casual sex defensible, a meagre 1 per cent of Chinese people think so.[152]

> Three in ten women and men could not locate the clitoris.[153]

> Only 2 per cent of men said they don't orgasm, while 20 per cent of women said they do not orgasm.[154]

> Three-quarters of women said they are unable to orgasm while having sex, while three in ten men said the best way to aid a woman to orgasm was via penetrative sexual actions.[155]

> In a 2019 study of Britons, 59 per cent of men and 45 per cent of women were unable to label the vagina.[156]

THE WINS

> Ann Summers parties, which began in 1981, helped de-stigmatise female sexual pleasure by encouraging women to buy vibrators, bringing sex toys to a much broader audience of revellers, some of whom may have felt too anxious to walk into a sex shop. Although the dimension of profit and sales intrinsic in such events cannot be naively overlooked.

> The infamous Rampant Rabbit vibrator – which emphasises clitoral stimulation via the ears – launched in 1991, rapidly selling every two minutes in the UK and still selling every three minutes today. The item is the world's most popular sex toy.[157]

> The Vagina Museum, dubbed the 'world's first bricks and mortar museum dedicated to the gynaecological anatomy', first opened in London in 2019 but is currently looking for a new home.

> All primary schools in England have been legally obliged to teach relationships education since 1 September 2020 after years of campaign work.

> The sex-positivity movement has a long history, but it had a rebirth in the sexual revolution of the 1960s and 1970s, as well as another renaissance in recent years.

> In 2002, the World Health Organization amended how it defines sexual health to also encompass pleasure.

RESOURCES

> Center for Positive Sexuality – Los Angeles-based organisation striving to tackle social issues via sex-positive research and education.

> Sexpression:UK – charity which provides informal and comprehensive relationships, sex and health education in the community.

> Brook – national sexual health charity for young people.

> Relate – biggest deliverer of relationship support in England and Wales which also provides sex therapy.

> Fumble – youth charity that provides free digital sex education resources and runs programmes in schools and universities.

11

TOXIC MASCULINITY

'I can't believe what you say, because
I see what you do.'

James Baldwin

Let's spell out what toxic masculinity is. It is a masculinity centred around aggression, dominance, clout and the suppression of vulnerable emotions. It is a negative social construct of a man, formed through decades of power imbalance, societal pressure and cultural conditioning. For me, a textbook 'cookie-cutter' toxic male would be a man who brags about his deadlifting in the gym, his ostentatious car and his sexual prowess, a man who treats his girlfriend or wife like a trophy he won and therefore owns; a man who appears ostensibly confident but then can grow inordinately incensed by any perceived slight to his ego, thus revealing that all is not what it seems. It is a man who struggles to express emotions which aren't anger, for fear he will not look strong or dominant. It is a man who often subscribes to black-and-white thinking, who lacks nuance and empathy in his approach, who struggles to admit and take responsibility for his own weaknesses. Of course, toxic masculinity doesn't always manifest in such a crudely clichéd way; it operates, like most things, on a sliding scale.

Toxic masculinity is a term that has been awarded some criticism of late – something that often happens when terminology mutates into a catch-all buzzword that pops up everywhere. Some argue we should steer clear of gendered notions of toxicity. Others warn the phrase unhelpfully fails to address the causes of toxic masculinity, while some, namely men's rights activists, find the term scandalously offensive and warn that it paints all men as inherently toxic.

For me, all of these criticisms fall woefully short and miss the point. The first piece of criticism about avoiding gendered ideas of toxicity feels too blindly utopian, given that, whether we like it or not, we live in a rigidly gendered world. Mark Brooks, chair of the ManKind Initiative, appears to be a proponent of this particular perspective. Brooks is eager to depart from gendered terms, telling *The Independent*, 'There is no such thing as toxic femininity – or toxic masculinity, for that matter. There [are] just toxic people and behaviour.'[158] His point makes sense in relation to toxic femininity – the term has no clear, universal definition – but, for me, it almost comically misses the point when it comes to toxic masculinity. It feels as though Brooks wrenches men from the cultural conditioning and societal structures in which they exist, also neglecting the unmistakable behavioural patterns and parallels that fall under toxic masculinity.

Brooks also argues that toxic masculinity is 'very anti-male and victim-blaming' and 'demonises a whole gender' – another view I take issue with. Shining a light on toxic masculinity does not mean you are saying masculinity is inherently toxic or that all men are toxic. On the contrary, it is about trying to decipher the deep-rooted cultural conditioning that has long plagued concepts of masculinity. Men as well as women are impacted negatively by the existence of toxic masculinity, with men often struggling to fit themselves into the rigid definitions of who they should be and how they should act. Brooks's view seems troublingly similar to those espoused by men's rights activists and trolls with too much time on their hands, who also hate the term toxic masculinity. These people remind me of the trope of someone yelling, 'I'm not angry!' while their forehead pulsates with rage yet cannot see the bitter irony of the situation. In other words, the very fact that some men are incensed by the term toxic masculinity goes some way to prove its existence. And perhaps it is partially their own privilege that blinds them to the prevalence of it.

There is more to this concept than armchair theorising, though. There are real-life consequences of toxic masculinity wielding its power, which are harmful for men themselves, as well as everyone else around them, and in the starkest circumstances they can even be deadly. In fact, a government safety campaign in France warned that toxic masculinity could be equally as dangerous as drink or drugs in contributing to road deaths – with the French government noting that men constituted a whopping 78 per cent of those killed on their roads in 2022, as well as making up 88 per cent of drivers aged between 18 and 24 killed on the road.[159] Meanwhile, men also made up 84 per cent of those suspected to have caused road accidents, and constituted 93 per cent of drunk drivers involved in an accident. The idea that your masculine prowess somehow overrides the alcohol swirling around your body would be a cautionary example of how damaging and even deadly toxic masculinity can be.

We must also consider the studies that reveal how boys and men with sexist views are more likely to commit gender-based violence and the fact that men perpetrate violent and sexual offences at substantially higher rates than women. Men's actions are also dramatically more likely to have fatal consequences.[160] Men are more likely to both kill others and kill themselves.[161] Let's not forget: almost every single US mass shooter since records began is a man. The Violence Project, which has recorded American mass-shooting figures from 1966, estimates that some 98 per cent of these crimes were perpetrated by men, and their research shows it is specifically white men who are the demographic most likely to engage in a mass shooting.[162]

To sum up, toxic masculinity cannot be used to make sense of all society's ills, but it is, nevertheless, alive, kicking and dangerous. It can be seen both as a symptom of wider patriarchal structures, but also as one element of the psychosocial glue that binds the patriarchy together. Phrases like 'man up', 'boys don't cry' and 'take it like a man' do not help matters. Instead, we must not only foster spaces for men to be open about their fears, as well as be emotional and vulnerable, but also hold displays of toxic masculinity – whether they are perpetrated by politicians, celebrities, acquaintances or loved ones – to account.

THE STATS

> More young men in the UK have seen material from Andrew Tate, a misogynistic influencer who has been dubbed 'the king of toxic masculinity', than have heard of the UK prime minister, Rishi Sunak.[163]

> Eight in ten boys aged between 16 and 17 had read, listened to or watched content from Tate; 45 per cent of men aged between 16 and 24 have a positive view of Tate, while only 26 per cent held a negative opinion of him. When probed about why they like Tate, most said they thought he 'wants men to be real men' or that 'he gives good advice'.[164]

> Six in ten young men in Britain said they feel pressured to 'man up', with almost seven in ten 18–24-year-olds feeling forced to show 'hyper-masculine' behaviour and just over half of young people saying a man would feel less masculine if he cried in front of other people.[165]

> Research found that toxic masculinity is preventing boys from pursuing help for their mental health – with almost four in ten boys and young men saying they are grappling with mental health issues but half being unable or reluctant to ask for support.[166]

> One study has found that male life expectancy in the Americas is almost six years below that of women. Researchers warn that societal pressures for men lead them to repress their emotions and engage in risk-taking behaviour which leads to higher rates among men of suicide, homicide, addiction issues and road accidents, and higher rates of chronic diseases such as heart disease, stroke, cancer and diabetes.[167]

RESOURCES

> Beyond Equality – working with men and boys to strive towards healthier masculinities and gender equality.

> Men at Work – training those working with young men and boys to help nurture healthy relationships and communities.

> Movember – prominent men's mental health charity.

> White Ribbon – charity which aims to end male violence against women.

> Equimundo: Center for Masculinities and Social Justice – working in the US and globally to facilitate boys and men to champion gender equality.

12

SEXUAL VIOLENCE

'You can survive rape. You never forget it – don't even
think that. But you can survive it and go on.'

Maya Angelou

The violence inflicted by a rapist has abundant ripple effects,
which many never think about. Across the world there are
adults who were conceived via rape, while there are also rape
victims who were forced to marry their perpetrators via 'marry
your rapist laws', or made to endure invasive, medically unsub-
stantiated vaginal examinations known as 'two-finger tests' in
a bid to potentially disprove their allegations. Meanwhile here
in the UK, sexual violence survivors routinely find themselves
trapped in wretched, unthinkable situations after they come
forward to report rape to the police, with some saying that
this process, and being dragged through the criminal justice
system, is worse than the incident of sexual violence itself.

There is a reason campaigners, experts and politicians have
all warned that rape has effectively been 'decriminalised' in the

UK. Prosecutions and convictions are pitiful, with rape long having the lowest charging rates of all crimes. A meagre 1.3 per cent of 67,125 rape offences recorded by police in 2021 resulted in a prosecution.[168] Rape Crisis England & Wales states only 1 out of 100 rapes recorded that year led to a charge – let alone a conviction.[169] Harmful rape myths abound, voiced everywhere from court rooms to the press, to the pub, to social media and in wider public discourse. They tend to blame rape on how women are dressed, on them 'flirting', on them drinking alcohol or on them simply leaving the house after dark. Sometimes it feels like the only thing you can do to elude victim-blaming as a woman is to sit at home, with all doors and windows locked.

Things have become so bad with rape in the UK that the government actually issued an overt apology to rape victims in summer 2021 as rape prosecutions hurtled to record lows in England and Wales. The government confessed that thousands of rape victims have been denied justice due to failings by police and prosecutors. 'The vast majority of victims do not see the crime against them charged and reach a court. One in two victims withdraw from rape investigations,' read a joint statement issued by the then home secretary, justice secretary and attorney general. 'These are trends of which we are deeply ashamed. Victims of rape are being failed. Thousands of victims have gone without justice.'[170]

Rape is a far more widespread issue than many realise. One in four women and one in eighteen men in England and Wales have been raped or sexually assaulted as an adult. Moreover, half of rapes against women are perpetrated by a partner or ex-partner, and five in six rapes against women are committed by an individual known to them, while men make up 98 per cent of adults prosecuted for serious sexual offences.[171] Despite all of these truths, it is worth noting that rape remains an invisible, hidden crime, as most victims never come forward to report it to the police. It is estimated that some five in six women and four in five men who are raped never report it.[172]

Dwindling trust in policing in the wake of a spate of scandals involving violent, sexually predatory officers is not helping matters. A story I covered revealed that half of women do not have faith in the police when it comes to assault claims. The report, led by Victim Support and shared exclusively with *The Independent*, discovered that 54 per cent of women lack confidence that the police will properly investigate their reports of domestic abuse, while 50 per cent said the same regarding sexual offences.[173] Overall, around four in ten women who have been the victim of a crime in the past two years said they felt let down by the police investigation into their case. The Casey Review into the Metropolitan Police, which is explored in greater detail in Chapter 7: Policing (see page 56), found that rape cases were dropped because DNA evidence was ruined when it was stored in 'over-stuffed, dilapidated or broken fridges and freezers' used by the Metropolitan Police.

Worryingly, the crippling court backlog gripping the UK is profoundly exacerbating many pre-existing issues with how the criminal justice system handles sexual violence cases. Unable to bear the delays, victims are dropping out of their cases. A story of mine published in *The Independent* in spring 2023 explored the fact that court backlogs for rape and sexual offences have hit a record high, with the most desperate victims driven to suicide by 'devastating' waits for justice. To put this into context, the logjam of cases in the crown courts skyrocketed to 7,859 sexual offence cases and 1,851 adult rape cases by September 2022.[174]

Research by Rape Crisis England & Wales tragically found that survivors of sexual violence are grappling with the longest delays of all crime victims, enduring an average wait of 839

'I AM NO LONGER

ACCEPTING

THE THINGS I CANNOT CHANGE.

I AM CHANGING

THE THINGS I

CANNOT ACCEPT'

ANGELA DAVIS

days from reporting the crime to a final court verdict.[175] Jayne Butler, the charity's chief executive, told me victims are sometimes totally unaware that their case is being postponed until they get to court. This doesn't bear thinking about. Imagine nervously getting dressed in your court-appropriate attire, riddled with anxiety about what is to come, only to arrive at court to be told to turn around and head straight back home. 'Victims aren't treated well,' Butler told me. 'They aren't told what is going on. They aren't prioritised by the system. This has to be the absolute rock bottom for the system. It can't possibly get any worse.'[176] For a long time, Rape Crisis has been calling for specialist courts for cases of sexual violence and abuse, in which the judges and court staff have undertaken trauma-informed training to make the process easier for victims.

It is also worth noting that the crisis in the over-capacity, understaffed prison system means that those men who do wind up being punished for their sex offences often aren't forced to tackle the behaviour that pushed them into prison in the first place. A joint probe by the inspectorates for police, prosecutors, prisons and probation found that 'people are leaving prison and/or finishing community sentences without addressing their offending behaviour' due to staff deficits.[177]

Outside the UK criminal justice system, rape is misunderstood and deprioritised. The heavy shame, stigma and blame that rape victims face can mean police investigations and trials are beset with a plethora of challenges. Research by Equality Now, a global NGO, found that the profoundly patriarchal view that only 'chaste' and 'moral' women and girls can be raped is commonplace in some parts of the world, with rape victims' sexual history being used against them and women routinely forced to provide highly discriminatory and invasive evidence.[178] The researchers who analysed six nations spanning from Bangladesh to Bhutan, Nepal, the Maldives, India and Sri Lanka warned that rape survivors and their families are pushed into informal community mediation, and also face victim-blaming, threats, bribery, being sacked or evicted, or yet more violence. Moreover, let's not forget, marital rape remains legal in many places in the world.

For good reason, the World Health Organisation describes violence perpetrated against women – namely domestic abuse and sexual violence – as a 'major public health problem' as well as a 'violation of women's human rights'.[179] The organisation estimates that some 30 per cent of women around the world have endured physical and/or sexual violence from a partner, or sexual violence from someone who is not their partner, at some point in their lives.

Of course, sexual violence does not always take the form of rape; sexual harassment remains rife in many walks of life. Polling by UN Women found that 97 per cent of young women in the UK said they had been sexually harassed, while 80 per cent reported experiencing sexual harassment in public spaces. Researchers polled more than 1,000 women aged between 18 and 24 and found that sexual harassment they'd experienced included being groped, followed and coerced into sexual activity.[180] What's more, sickeningly enough, research by Plan International found that just over one in three girls in the UK has been sexually harassed in their school uniform.[181] Sexual violence comes in a glut of configurations and is something that, sadly, far too many women have experienced.

THE STATS

> Black women have been found to be three times more likely to sign a non-disclosure agreement (NDA) – legal contracts routinely wielded to silence survivors of sexual harassment,

violence, bullying or other misconduct in workplaces – than white women.[182]

> Research has found in cases where NDAs were used involving sexual harassment allegations, 29 per cent of women reported signing an NDA, substantially more than 18 per cent of men.[183]

> In England and Wales, 6.5 million women are estimated to have been raped or sexually assaulted.[184]

> One in thirty women is raped or sexually assaulted each year in England and Wales.[185]

> Police forces are failing to protect abuse victims by not using existing powers to tackle domestic violence, rape, harassment and stalking, the Centre for Women's Justice has warned.[186]

> Police units dealing with domestic abuse and sexual offences are 'chronically under-resourced', and police guidance, training and supervision need to be improved, the Centre for Women's Justice states.[187]

> Concerns have been raised that fresh Crown Prosecution Service (CPS) guidance released in May 2022 will prevent rape survivors from getting counselling and therapy, as the recommendations increase the chances that prosecutors will retrieve therapy records of rape survivors in a bid to undermine them in court.[188]

> Rape investigations are hampered by police not believing women who report crimes and by officers perpetrating 'victim-blaming' in England and Wales, with some believing that most reports of rape are merely cases of 'regretful sex', according to a report for the National Police Chiefs' Council and the Home Office.[189]

> Two-thirds of girls aged between 14 and 21 in the UK have altered their behaviour to protect themselves from sexual harassment in public spaces, such as avoiding exercise and even going to school due to being anxious about being harassed.[190]

> The World Health Organisation estimates that around the world almost one in three women has endured physical and/or sexual violence from their partner, or sexual violence not perpetrated by a partner, at some point in their life.[191]

RESOURCES

> Rape Crisis England & Wales – membership organisation for 39 Rape Crisis centres that provides support to those impacted by sexual violence.

> Can't Buy My Silence – campaigning to stop non-disclosure agreements being wielded to silence victims.

> End Violence against Women Coalition – leading umbrella organisation.

> The Survivors Trust – UK's biggest umbrella network for specialist rape and sexual abuse services.

> Women against Rape – grassroots organisation helping survivors of sexual violence.

> Rights of Women – charity which provides free legal advice for women who have suffered sexual harassment at work among other services.

13

MENTAL HEALTH

'Men often ask me, Why are your female characters
so paranoid? It's not paranoia. It's recognition
of their situation.'

Margaret Atwood

It is often said that conversations about mental health have
come on in leaps and bounds in recent years – a statement that
has genuine merit, but also one that is only true if you define
mental health in narrow, exclusionary terms. Yes, anxiety and
depression are less taboo than they were just a few years ago,
but I'm not sure if the same can be said for bipolar, psychosis,
schizophrenia, personality disorders and other lesser-known
mental illnesses.

While the latter list remains profoundly stigmatised for all,
women grappling with these mental illnesses endure a special
kind of shame. This might be because in many ways society
holds women to higher standards than men. When a man
becomes incensed and lashes out, it is less frowned upon than

when a woman does the same. This probably has something to do with the fact that it is substantially more common for men to be outwardly physically aggressive than women, but it may also be linked to how history has long considered women's rage unnerving and dangerous.

This was particularly true in the eighteenth and nineteenth centuries when 'female hysteria' was one of the most frequently diagnosed disorders. Everything but the kitchen sink was interpreted as an indication of female hysteria – with symptoms ranging from infertility to a penchant for writing, increased or decreased sex drive, depression, overt displays of emotion, chest pain and more. It was thought that hysteria was precipitated by issues with the uterus. In fact, the very word hysteria is gendered, deriving from the Latin word *hystericus*, which means 'of the womb'. Marriage, herbs, having leeches placed on the abdomen, sex, celibacy and forced orgasm were among the bizarre and inhumane forms of treatment offered to alleviate purported hysteria. During this time women were shunned, hidden away in 'insane asylums', and tortured and mistreated in the hunt for cures to their 'mania'.

While things have fortunately come a long way since then, it does sometimes feel like we are quicker to diagnose women and label them as mentally ill than men. Women are more likely to be diagnosed with borderline personality disorder, with some health professionals arguing that misogynistic bias can result in misdiagnoses.[192] But women are also overrepresented with other mental health problems. Across the globe, women are more likely to be diagnosed with depression and anxiety, and while the overall suicide rate for men is considerably higher than it is for women, women are more likely than men to attempt suicide.

Nevertheless, it is hard to gauge the veracity of the disproportionate number of women diagnosed with anxiety and depression, given that we know women are more likely to seek help for both physical and mental health problems. Saying that, my instinctive feeling, as a journalist with a keen interest in mental health but who obviously isn't a mental health expert, is that women on the whole are more likely to experience anxiety than men. This is because women seem to internalise their problems more and turn pain inwards on themselves, endlessly and often needlessly ruminating, while men seem more likely to externalise their neuroses, becoming angry and perhaps even violent, or self-medicating with alcohol or drugs.

Societal factors offer up another major reason why women may be more predisposed to mental health problems than men. Research by the University of Manchester discovered that individuals with borderline personality disorder were 13 times more likely to report childhood abuse than those who do not have a mental illness, while there is a slew of other statistics showing a correlation between women's mental health and violence and abuse (research has found that 53 per cent of women who have mental health problems have endured abuse).[193] However, this is an issue that appears to be overlooked; research suggests that mental health services are 'putting women at risk' by failing to ask them about their experience of domestic abuse. Agenda Alliance, a charity that campaigns for women and girls at risk, has found that more than a third of NHS mental health trusts are failing to ask women about domestic abuse in spite of recommended guidelines.[194]

To put it simply, it is important to remember that mental health does not exist in a vacuum. On the contrary, our inner worlds hold up a mirror to our own personal life experiences and to wider society. We all have differing degrees of trauma and differing responses to it. What's more, mental health cannot be extricated from material wealth, with research finding that those in poverty are more likely to contend with poor mental health.[195]

A major concern for all is that mental healthcare in the NHS has been historically and chronically underfunded and is presently in crisis mode, with the longest waiting times in decades. Meanwhile, a recent inquiry found that young people experiencing serious mental health conditions were sometimes being denied NHS treatment until they could demonstrate that they had made 'multiple suicide attempts with serious intent'.

Nevertheless, the plight of those suffering from acute mental health issues in the UK often remains obscured from view and thus neglected. It also continues to be sanitised in social media spheres, with harsh, uncomfortable realities swept under the rug. After all, unless you or a loved one have serious mental health issues, have been voluntarily or involuntarily sectioned, or you or someone you know works inside a psychiatric unit, it is likely you will have little idea of what mental health can look like at its worst or what the services people encounter are like. Psychiatric units remain something of an enigma to those outside their highly securitised walls. Being violently restrained by multiple members of staff to be forcibly injected with powerful medication or being isolated in seclusion rooms are just some of the routine practices in psychiatric units for those patients who infringe the uncompromising rules in place. Sadly, data demonstrates that it is the women residing in psychiatric units who are substantially more likely than their male counterparts to have chemicals forcibly injected while being restrained by staff.[196]

This is an issue I have written about previously, as is electric shock therapy – a type of treatment that many people I speak to assume stopped being administered in the 1980s. Electroconvulsive therapy (ECT), the formal name, involves around 10 sessions, with electricity passed through the brain to cause a seizure in each session. In an investigation for *The Independent*, I revealed that thousands of women were being given ECT despite concerns that it can cause irreversible brain damage; the story shone a light on the fact that ECT is prescribed disproportionately to women, who constituted around two-thirds of all patients in 2019.[197] Experts told me how the severe side effects can leave patients unable to recognise family and friends or do basic maths. Nevertheless, it is worth noting that some patients say ECT has helped their condition, while the Department of Health and Social Care states that the treatment can help individuals for whom other therapies have failed.

With all of this in mind, it can feel like we haven't moved as far beyond the 'mental asylums' of the eighteenth and nineteenth centuries than we might sometimes assume. Research shows that people's mental health around the world is worsening; the World Health Organization estimates that some 5 per cent of adults experience depression, warning that it has become the 'leading cause of disability worldwide'.[198] In the UK and the US, the number of antidepressants doctors dish out is on the rise. The solution? Like most things, it is complex. What's more, it is as much about alleviating the malaise of the world around us, as it is about rectifying our own personal neuroses.

We live in turbulent times. Climate change, the refugee crisis, Covid-19, the Russia–Ukraine war, the rise of the far right and the energy crisis are just some of the major geopolitical events currently unleashing havoc. Reasonably priced, accessible psychotherapy for all would help matters tremendously – something there is a dramatic dearth of around the world. Instead, here in the UK and in other countries, we routinely over-medicalise, excessively label and pathologise those suffering from mental health issues. These quick-fix solutions are often akin to sticking a cursory plaster over a gaping wound.

THE STATS

> Women are more likely to be diagnosed with depression, anxiety, borderline personality disorder and PTSD than men.[199]

> Girls have much higher rates of self-harm than boys in the UK, while young women's rates of self-harm have more than tripled since the 1990s.[200]

> Women living in poverty are more likely to experience poor mental health – 29 per cent endure a common mental health disorder in comparison to 16 per cent of women not living in poverty.[201]

> Women are more than twice as likely as men to be given a diagnosis of anxiety and prescribed medication, including antidepressants, to alleviate symptoms.[202]

> Hundreds of thousands more women than men in England have been prescribed powerful anti-anxiety drugs called benzodiazepines (better known by the brand names of Valium, Xanax and Temazepam), which experts warn are harder to come off than heroin.[203]

> Coronavirus chaos worsened the existing gender inequalities in mental health, with women's wellbeing disproportionately affected by the pandemic – and young women faring worst.[204]

> Around the world women are more likely to attempt suicide, yet the overall suicide rate for men is considerably higher

than it is for women.[205]

> Black women are more likely to be sectioned in mental health units and to be restrained once inside them than white women.[206]

> Men are less likely to go to therapy or seek professional help for mental health issues than women.[207]

> Women face extra hurdles in battling addiction because male-focused drug support services neglect their needs, with many women finding addiction support services daunting and intimidating.[208]

> Women who are domestic abuse victims are three times more likely to try to kill themselves, study finds.[209]

> The World Health Organisation states nearly 1 in 5 women will endure a mental health condition while going through pregnancy or in the year that follows childbirth – with 2 in 10 women grappling with perinatal mental health issues having suicidal thoughts or self-harming.[210]

THE WINS

> More high-profile individuals have spoken publicly about their own struggles with mental health issues in recent years, which helps to reduce the stigma.

> A December 2017 court ruling considered changes to Personal Independence Payments as 'blatantly discriminatory' to individuals with mental illness and required the government to review and backdate many payments. The government revealed it would not challenge the ruling in January 2018.

> The government passed Seni's Law in 2018, to curb the use of restraint in mental health settings. The law is named after Olaseni Lewis, a 23-year-old British man, who died in 2010 at Bethlem Royal Hospital in London after six police officers restrained him for more than 30 minutes using 'excessive' force. Lewis, who had voluntarily accessed support and care after suffering from mental health problems, passed away three days after the restraint took place.

> Seni's Law means police must wear body cameras when attending a mental health unit.

> The government established in law the idea that mental health must get the same priority as physical health via the Health and Social Care Act 2012 – this is called 'parity of esteem'.

RESOURCES

> Free Psychotherapy Network – provides free psychotherapy for those on low incomes and benefits.

> Sorry My Mental Illness Isn't Sexy Enough for You – a platform for those with the most 'stigmatised and misunderstood mental health disorders' to share personal stories.

> Samaritans – delivers support to anyone in emotional distress or feeling suicidal in the UK and Ireland via its helpline.

> Campaign against Living Miserably – raises awareness of suicide and funds a free, anonymous, confidential helpline.

> YoungMinds – a mental health charity for children, young people and their parents.

> MindOut – a mental health service run by and for LGBTQ+ individuals.

> British Association for Counselling and Psychotherapy – professional talking therapy and counselling organisation, which has a list of accredited therapists.

> Black Minds Matter UK – UK charity that links up Black individuals and families with free mental health services.

> The Black, African and Asian Therapy Network – the UK's biggest community of psychotherapists and counsellors of Black, African, Asian and Caribbean heritage.

> Find a Helpline – a database of free, confidential support helplines as well as online chat services around the world.

14

SEX WORK

'I believe feminism is grounded in supporting the choices of women even if we wouldn't make certain choices for ourselves.'

Roxane Gay

People might sell sex for an abundance of different reasons, but their motivations are routinely glossed over. These include, among others, being pushed into selling sex due to poverty, being coerced into prostitution by a pimp or trafficker, or a personal inclination to pursue sex work. Ironically and worryingly, it is this last motivating factor that people are often most likely to fixate on and find most distressing to come to terms with. As such, they seek to deny this reasoning and instead pontificate about why prostitution can never be a free or rational choice that someone would make.

Debates about sex work – an industry where women make up the majority of the workforce – are fiercely ideological and emotionally charged. Like a proverbial onion, there are many layers and complexities to the questions surrounding prostitution. What can begin as a conversation about sex work can quickly descend into a fiery dispute about liberalism, morality and capitalism. Feminists take dramatically different approaches to sex work, and I would label it as the most divisive issue of all in feminism. While transgender rights may have usurped sex work in their ability to polarise and alienate in recent years, this remains a fairly new phenomenon.

Sadly, it is not hard for the question of whether people should be allowed to buy and sell sex to spiral into counterproductively fraught and antagonistic debates. Those individuals who are opposed to sex work (who of course operate on a spectrum) passionately, almost viscerally, argue against prostitution from a moral perspective, with some feminists seeing it as a cause and symptom of patriarchy, and something that ultimately bolsters the oppression of women. Anti-sex-work feminists deem the act of exchanging sex for money as inherently violent, exploitative and unjust. This is despite the fact that studies consistently show that when sex work is criminalised, violence and abuse towards sex workers rises.[211]

Moreover, it always strikes me as profoundly hypocritical when you see feminists shout 'my body, my choice' as they campaign for abortion rights yet remain fiercely opposed to sex work. While, of course, sex work and abortion are distinct issues of very different natures, presumably if you believe women and people of diverse genders should have the right to choose to keep or terminate a pregnancy, you also think they should have agency and autonomy over whether they decide to sell sex. However, that is not the case, with a sizeable number of feminists remaining fervently pro-abortion rights while passionately opposed to sex work.

In the UK, the law around sex work is complex and can be hard to get your head around. While it might not be illegal for individuals to buy or sell sex in the UK, many of the activities that sex work necessitates are illegal: soliciting, working on the street, sex workers banding together as a group and prostitutes advertising themselves are all against the law. In criminalising more than one sex worker operating from a premises, the law denies them a critical mechanism they can use to remain safe from dangerous customers.

But let's return to the question of why you might choose to do sex work. Poverty cannot be overlooked. This is an issue I have explored a lot in my role as women's correspondent, writing about increasing numbers of public sector workers being forced to turn to sex work due to austerity measures and welfare cuts, sex workers being left penniless and facing homelessness during the Covid-19 crisis, and the cost-of-living crisis pushing many women into sex work for the first time or forcing them to return to it after stopping for many years.[212]

A major issue that plagues sex work is ignorant misconceptions about who sells sex. In short, sex workers are not who many people assume they are. They are mothers, girlfriends, wives, teachers, nurses and public sector workers, and are often juggling sex work with another job of some kind. Nevertheless, sex workers arguably fall victim to more vicious stereotyping than those in any other profession. When many picture a sex worker, they think of women doing street-based sex work to feed their drug addiction or long-limbed, high-end female escorts chaperoning businessmen. In fairness, this is because these are the images of sex workers that are most firmly embedded in public consciousness.

Such stereotyping can also be attributed to the strong sense of shame that has long tainted perceptions of prostitution – which is no doubt compounded by the underground, shadowy nature of the work. It is tricky to ascertain how many people do sex work because people don't want to be open about their

'I BELIEVE FEMINISM IS GROUNDED IN

SUPPORTING THE CHOICES OF WOMEN

EVEN IF WE WOULDN'T MAKE CERTAIN CHOICES FOR OURSELVES.'

– Roxane Gay

profession for fear of facing arrest, prosecution or stigma. Interestingly, however, a 2015 report by Leeds University funded by the Wellcome Trust discovered that more than 70 per cent of UK sex workers previously worked in healthcare, education or the charity sector.[213]

Another subject area I've written about a lot is violence perpetrated against sex workers. While harassment and violence against women and girls are prevalent in all walks of life, sex workers are particularly vulnerable, with research finding that women who sell sex are 18 times more likely to be murdered than women who don't.[214] Sex workers I've interviewed over the years have told me about violent attacks from customers as well as horrendous encounters with the police where they are accused of spurious allegations, intimidated and slut-shamed. For these reasons and more, sex workers themselves, as well as the campaign groups that support them, say the same thing again and again: they want sex work to be decriminalised.

This is a position many prestigious organisations agree with: Amnesty International, the World Health Organization, UNAIDS, the American Civil Liberties Union and the Royal College of Nursing are all calling for sex work to be decriminalised. They argue that this will boost sex workers' safety and access to healthcare, as well as opening more routes to leave prostitution (particularly by not putting sex workers in a position where they feel unable to leave the profession due to acquiring a criminal record) and improving wider sexual health. It goes without saying a criminal record not only can make it hard to find work but can have repercussions on access to housing too. Arguments for decriminalisation feel increasingly pressing in the context of the cost-of-living crisis gripping the UK. Speaking to me for a story in November 2022, campaigners explained how spiralling living costs are endangering sex workers' safety by forcing them to accept potentially dangerous male clients whose inquiries they would previously have rejected.[215]

Niki Adams, a spokesperson for the English Collective of Prostitutes, a leading campaign group that supports the decriminalisation of prostitution, often tells me that most sex workers never report violent and abusive incidents to the police due to being terrified that they will face arrest, prosecution, eviction from their home, having their kids removed and put into care or in some cases deportation. Moreover, the criminalisation of sex workers forces women to resort to working alone, or in more isolated areas, such as industrial estates or parks, where they are at far greater risk of violence.

A key approach to sex work adopted by certain countries is referred to as the Nordic Model. So christened after it was first introduced in Sweden, this model claims to punish the buyers of sex work while decriminalising sex workers themselves. Some feminists are massively in favour of the Nordic Model, but while this is an approach that may seem appealing to the untrained eye, many experts, campaigners and sex workers themselves are stridently opposed to it, due to research finding that it increases violence against sex workers, as well as making it hard to screen out potentially dangerous clients. Ireland introduced the Nordic Model in 2017, and it is also the model employed in Sweden, France and Norway.

In the US, the selling and purchase of sex is illegal, yet there is no overarching nationwide law banning sex work. Instead, the intricacies of legislation oscillate wildly between states and sometimes even between cities. Moreover, sex work is legal in some counties in Nevada. Shockingly, some individuals arrested for carrying out sex work in Louisiana were made to register as sex offenders up until 2011.[216] Meanwhile, 2018 book *Revolting Prostitutes: The Fight for Sex Workers' Rights* notes sex workers arrested around the US are sometimes imprisoned until they go to trial if they cannot afford to pay their bail.[217]

Rachel West, who works for an American sex worker rights group called US PROStitutes Collective, told me criminalisation has a 'devastating effect on sex workers' and is particularly tough on mothers with families to look after. 'If we are convicted and especially if we end up in jail, we risk losing custody of our children,' she added. 'In jail we can be detained before trial if we can't afford to post bail, impacting mostly those of us who are Black and Latinx. Criminalisation also forces sex workers into more dangerous work environments. Violent men are encouraged to attack with impunity because our lives are devalued and we are deterred from reporting violence for fear of arrest.'

Sex work might repeatedly be referred to as 'the world's oldest profession', but it is not without complexities. As such, it is important not to take a lazily libertarian 'it is what it is' approach, which either disregards problems with the industry or glamorises women making money from sex. But on the other hand, criminalising sex work and subsequently pushing it underground helps nothing and nobody; instead, it inflicts needless terror and distress on its workforce.

THE STATS

> Sex work refers not only to prostitution but also to webcam models, strippers, phone sex operators and more.

> While women make up the majority of sex workers, the industry also encompasses many men and gender-diverse individuals.

> Research has found that violence and threats of deportation against sex workers from the European Union who are

living in the UK have surged since the Brexit vote, with 44 per cent of EU migrant sex workers experiencing an increase in the levels of violence they endure.[218]

> Around seven in ten police raids that the media reported on as being linked to modern slavery and sex trafficking are not resulting in any trafficking victims being referred to support services, new data shows.[219]

> Research has found reports of violence and rape are far more common among street-based sex workers than those who work inside.[220]

> One study has found that more people in Britain support sex work law reform than oppose it, with 49 per cent in favour of decriminalising brothel-keeping – an offence punishable by up to seven years in prison.[221]

> Tens of thousands of individuals are 'arrested, prosecuted, incarcerated, deported, or fined' for offences linked to sex work in the US each year.[222]

> Almost 40 per cent of adults and 60 per cent of young people arrested for prostitution in the US in 2015 were Black.[223]

> Statistics from Ugly Mugs – an app where sex workers can confidentially report incidents of abuse and crime – state that the number of such incidents being reported has greatly increased since Ireland banned the purchase of sexual services. They say crime against sex workers has increased 90 per cent, while violent crime specifically has increased by 92 per cent.[224]

THE WINS

> More than 200 prostitutes marched on the Central Methodist Church in San Francisco to show their opposition to a campaign opposed to prostitution fronted by the church's pastor in 1917.

> The term 'sex work' was established by an activist called Carol Leigh somewhere between the late 1970s and early '80s.

> Sex workers and campaigners protested about sex workers being murdered by the Yorkshire Ripper at a 1981 picket of the High Court in London.

> Sex workers from around the world set up the Global Network of Sex Work Projects (NSWP) in 1990 at the second International AIDS Conference in the French capital of Paris.

> Two sex workers brought the first successful private prosecution for rape in 1995 – with the backing of the English Collective of Prostitutes and Women against Rape.

> Over 25,000 sex workers came together in India for a festival launched by a Calcutta-based group called the Durbar Mahila Samanwaya Committee in 2001, even though the government bowed to a backlash and withdrew the parade's permit – this gathering laid the groundwork for International Sex Workers' Rights Day, which falls on 3 March.

> New Zealand decriminalised sex work in 2003.

> Campaigners came together to resist mass police raids in Soho in central London in 2013.

RESOURCES

> Global Mapping of Sex Work Laws – map showing different sex work laws around the world created by the Global Network of Sex Work Projects (NSWP).

> Ugly Mugs – an app where sex workers can confidentially report incidents of abuse and crime.

> English Collective of Prostitutes – leading grassroots organisation which supports sex workers and campaigns for the decriminalisation of prostitution.

> Hookers against Hardship – a coalition of sex worker organisations calling for the suspension of evictions, as well as an amnesty from arrest for sex workers to ensure that women can report violence without fear in the UK.

> Sonagachi project – a sex work rights project in India, which tackles HIV prevention and champions condom use.

> International Day to End Violence against Sex Workers (17 December) – day to raise awareness of violence and hate crimes perpetrated against sex workers around the world.

15

PRISONS

'The majority of people who are in prison are there
because society has failed them.'

Angela Davis

Prison is often akin to state-sanctioned trauma, neglect, abuse
and even torture. Ostensibly, that might sound extreme to
some, but if you have had any experience of prison, or known
anyone who has, you will know how it stands up. Watertight.
Clear as day. While the prison guard is not reclining on a
chair with their feet perched on the table stubbing cigarette
butts out on your forehead or engaging in the traditional
torture methods you see in films, the reality is no less harmful
and degrading. Imprisonment can involve being locked
in your cell for up to 23 hours a day, being blocked from
attending necessary and even life-saving healthcare appoint-
ments, and being isolated from family, friends and the wider
community. Research has found that prison accelerates the
ageing process, shortens life expectancy and makes anyone

inside increasingly vulnerable to illness, disease and mental health issues.

But where do women come into this? While the whole prison population is a highly vulnerable demographic, the situation is far starker for female prisoners. Experts warn that women in prison are often victims of radically more serious crimes than the ones they have been convicted of. Research by the Prison Reform Trust found that 80 per cent of women in prison in the UK were serving sentences for non-violent offences.[225] To give you a sense of how this plays out, TV licence evasion was the offence that had the largest share of female defendants in 2021, with women making up as many as three-quarters of those prosecuted for TV licence evasion.[226] This petty, negligible offence, which many Britons probably don't even realise is criminalised, made up a whopping 18 per cent of all female prosecutions.

On top of this, stealing from shops was the most frequent indictable offence for women defendants in 2021, making up 21 per cent of all female prosecutions for indictable offences, which is a sizeable amount, especially when compared to the 8 per cent for men.[227] In other words, just as we often judge women more harshly than men in other walks of life, the same happens in the criminal justice system.

To put it super simply, and albeit a bit crudely, society expects better of women. A man commits a petty crime, and he is a lovable rogue or a bit of a bad boy, whereas a woman perpetrates a crime and we are more likely to stigmatise her, 'other' her and vilify her. A quote from Dr Rachel Tynan, of Unlock, a criminal justice charity, remains firmly lodged in my head. 'It is not that men aren't stigmatised, but men and women are stigmatised in different ways,' she said. 'There is a narrative for the bad boy gone good. That does not exist for women. Popular culture doesn't tell the story of the routes to redemption for women like it does for men.'[228]

'THE MOST COMMON WAY PEOPLE GIVE UP THEIR POWER IS BY THINKING THEY DON'T HAVE ANY.'

– Alice Walker

Often dubbed a 'minority within a minority', women prisoners only make up around 5 per cent of the prison population and 15 per cent of those doing a community sentence.[229] Manifold studies have discovered that a sizeable proportion of the female prison population endured domestic and childhood abuse, while many suffer from mental health issues. Around half of female prisoners report experiencing anxiety and depression, in comparison to just under a quarter of male prisoners.[230] Meanwhile, 53 per cent of women embroiled in the criminal justice system say they were abused as children, in comparison to 27 per cent of men.[231] What's more, depressingly, Ministry of Justice data shows almost half of all female prisoners in England and Wales say they carried out their offence to aid another person's drug habit. Once in jail, women are also radically more likely to self-harm than their male counterparts.

Many of these UK trends are mirrored on a global scale, with research finding that women and girls constitute around 7 per cent of the world prison population. The fifth edition of the World Female Imprisonment List found that there are more than 740,000 women and girls imprisoned around the world, while the female prison population has been rising far more quickly than the male population since 2000. Although the global male prison population has risen by around 22 per cent during this time, this is marginal compared to the 60 per cent jump for imprisoned women and girls.[232]

Unsurprisingly, America has the most women in prison per 100,000 people in the wider population. This is followed by Thailand, El Salvador, Turkmenistan and Brunei Darussalam. 'The sustained and substantial rise in the numbers of women and girls in prison across much of the world is a cause of profound concern,' states Helen Fair, who is behind the World Female Imprisonment List alongside Roy Walmsley at Birkbeck's Institute for Crime and Justice Policy Research. 'It has long been recognised that most female prisoners are extremely vulnerable – with histories of poverty, mental illness and sexual and physical victimisation. Their incarceration makes little contribution to public safety, while imposing high financial and social costs.'[233]

This quote, of course, has much resonance here in the UK. Make no mistake, despite the smaller numbers, we do like to lock people up and throw away the proverbial key in this country. Research by the Council of Europe found we spend more on jails in England and Wales than any other European country besides Russia.[234] The total budget was a liberal £3.4 billion in 2019, with our spending significantly rising since 2015. To put this into context, Germany forks out £3 billion and France spends £2.5 billion, despite having much bigger populations. In spite of the size of our population, the UK has the third-biggest prison population after Russia, which is followed by Turkey.

Jail in the UK is a hidden, forgotten place, with the prison estate and the humans who inhabit it shrouded and oppressed by their invisibility. Prisoners rarely have a voice. The metaphor of a car with blacked-out windows springs to mind because in many ways prisoners have substantial insight into what is going on in the outside world – via consuming the news, going on the internet on smart phones smuggled into prisons and interactions with loved ones during visits and phone calls – whereas many non-prisoners are clueless about the inner machinations of the prison population. Sadly, for many, being behind bars is akin to being out of sight, out of mind. In my view, this is why gross human rights abuses in the prison population are able to run wild.

This hit home when I wrote an article for *VICE* about pregnancy in prison entitled 'Babies behind Bars' back in 2015 and I was staggered to see how little had been written about this issue – there was the silence and invisibility in action. This is a subject area I've continued to write about at *The Independent*, with the issue garnering growing attention and outrage in recent years due to the hard work of campaigners. In my view, prison is not a place where pregnant women should be.

Two babies recently died behind bars in England. In 2020, there was a 31-year-old woman who gave birth to a stillborn baby in the toilet in Styal prison in Cheshire after a nurse incorrectly claimed her stomach cramps were due to a 'painful period'. She was not given specialist medical care or pain relief while going through the ordeal of labour. In another equally heartbreaking case, an 18-year-old woman saw her baby die in childbirth at Bronzefield prison in Surrey in 2019 after she was left to give birth alone in her prison cell, despite having asked for help a number of times.

A woman I interviewed previously for *The Independent*, who was pregnant in prison in the UK, told me at one point she was sleeping in a double room on a top bunk. She also said her single bed got more uncomfortable as her bump got bigger, as she warned she 'could feel metal planks lying underneath my body', while all she had to cover herself were 'thin blankets'.[235] She told me of how she was imprisoned for six months on remand and denied bail twice while pregnant. 'Prison is not good for the health of the baby,' she said. 'They cannot meet your health or social needs. The babies are not prisoners. You hear horror stories of prison officers assisting live births when they are not medically trained.' The woman, who was separated from her other child while in prison, was later found not guilty and released.

Research from Nuffield Health in 2020 found that one in ten imprisoned women gives birth inside prison or en route to the hospital.[236] Although female inmates are legally allowed to keep their babies for the first 18 months in a secure mother-and-baby prison unit, many children born in prison are separated from their mothers once born. Mahatma Gandhi, eminent Indian lawyer and activist famed for non-violent resistance, powerfully stated that 'the true measure of any society can be found in how it treats its most vulnerable members'. Surely pregnant female prisoners are some of the most vulnerable people in society, and it is clear we are not treating them with respect, dignity or compassion. The four walls of a prison cell are not fit for adult men and women, so they are certainly not the right environment for a pregnant mother, an unborn child or a newborn.

THE STATS

> Ministry of Justice data shows that almost half of all female prisoners in England and Wales say they committed their offence to support the drug use of someone else.[237]

> Women often serve shorter prison sentences than men due to being convicted for more minor offences, with 17 per cent of women and 7 per cent of men serving sentences of less than a year as of June 2022.[238]

> Women accounted for 22 per cent of all self-harm incidents in prison in 2021 even though they constituted just 4 per cent of the prison population.[239] The number who self-harmed per 1,000 inmates was 350 for women and 135 for men.[240]

> Over half the women imprisoned say they have endured domestic abuse.[241]

› There were, on average, 29 pregnant women in jail per week in 2021/22 – with 50 births taking place in a year.[242]

› Research has found that pregnant women in jail are five times more likely to endure a stillbirth than women in the non-prison population.[243]

› Women made up 4 per cent of the prison estate as of June 2022, with men constituting 96 per cent – this gender gap has been consistent for the last half a decade.[244]

› The US has the highest imprisonment rate in the world, with almost two million people in prison.[245]

› In the US, the women's prison population was over six times higher in 2021 than it was in 1980, surging from 26,326 to 168,449.[246]

› The speed of growth for incarcerated women has been twice as high as for the male prison population in the US since 1980.[247]

› The number of Black women jailed in the US – 62 per 100,000 – was far higher than the number of white women – 38 per 100,000 – in 2021.[248]

› In the US, 25 per cent of women in prison have been convicted of a drug offence, in comparison to 12 per cent of men.[249]

RESOURCES

› Women in Prison – charity helping women impacted by the criminal justice system and campaigning to end prison's damaging repercussions.

> Clean Break – theatre company launched by two women in prison using theatre to raise awareness of women in prison.

> Working Chance – the UK's only employment charity only helping women with convictions.

> Koestler Arts – striving to inspire prisoners, as well as those in secure hospitals and detention centres, to participate in the arts.

> Unlock – criminal justice charity helping those with criminal records to move forward with their lives.

> Prison Reform Trust – charity seeking to create a more fair and humane penal system.

> Amnesty International – prominent human rights organisation helping female political prisoners around the world.

16

BODY IMAGE PRESSURE

'It is not my job to please them with my body.'

Roxane Gay

As someone born in the year the Soviet Union collapsed, the Rampant Rabbit arrived on shelves and Nirvana's iconic *Nevermind* album was released, I would consider myself a precursor to the digital native generation. But 1991 was not just a milestone moment for geopolitics, women's sexual pleasure and grunge rock, it was also a seismic time for the World Wide Web, with the world introduced to its first ever website on 6 August (two days after I was born). Needless to say, this did not mean the internet was a big feature of my childhood – something I am eternally grateful for given that teenage body image pressures felt punishing enough without Instagram and TikTok to contend with. The prospect of navigating a changing body amid raging hormones in a sea of picture-perfect bodies on social media to compare your angst-ridden teenage self to is daunting, to say the least.

While it is difficult to say for certain, it feels as though body image pressures have become particularly omnipresent in recent years, and the data backs this up, with young people among the most vulnerable casualties. While there are, of course, benefits to growing up online, research consistently finds that body image issues are acutely felt among younger generations. One in six girls and young women in Britain had not attended school or their workplace in the past year because they were anxious about the way they look, according to one study. The research, carried out by development charity Plan International, which I covered at the time, reported that nine in ten girls feel a burden to tally up to an 'ideal' type of face and physique, and a quarter feel 'ashamed or disgusted' by their body.[250] Troublingly, over a quarter were found to have not left the house and a fifth to have avoided public speaking due to such anxieties in the last year.

It can sometimes feel like body image pressure is dismissed as a fluffy, overstated issue, which only affects a minority of people. Or something that is located in people's heads that doesn't have tangible real-world consequences. These statistics annihilate those views, showing that body image woes can radically impact the way someone lives their life, destroying their wellbeing and subsequently impinging on their freedom. While body image pressure sometimes felt unavoidable as a teenager, I cannot help feeling grateful that I was shielded from the immaculately curated bikini-clad bodies of Instagram influencers. It may not be helpful to fall prey to naive nostalgia, but the days and nights spent exploring the streets and park benches of London with friends were a helpful distraction from body image worries.

Of course, young people still excel at roaming the streets now, and some degree of body image anxiety feels like an inherent part of teenage life, but there is no disputing the fact that young people today spend far more time on social media than previous generations, who simply didn't have these apps at their disposal. After all, going online was previously far more of a chore, as it involved waiting around for the dial-up modem to connect. Perhaps tellingly, many of the low points of being a teenager were the times spent online. Bullying felt rife on MSN Messenger, while social anxiety felt inescapable on MySpace.

To turn to the broader issue of body image pressure, though, it seems important to highlight that in commodifying bodies and faces to sell stuff, we twist and warp humans into idealised entities. Shiny images of beautiful, slim women and muscular, rugged men are everywhere you look. Whether they are plastered on billboards or pop up on adverts on your TV, laptop, social media feed or in magazines, they can be hard to escape. Bags under the eyes, oversized pores and shiny foreheads are touched up and omitted via Photoshop or an equivalent program. In turn, we are left transfixed by models who look almost ethereal and otherworldly due to having been so starkly airbrushed and doctored.

Some politicians think there should be greater transparency over this, with MPs calling on the government to do more to stop social media users' body image woes by rolling out a law ensuring that digitally doctored 'commercial images' of bodies have labels on them indicating that they have been tinkered with. MPs who sit on the Health and Social Care Select Committee in the House of Commons previously issued a plea to ministers to take the repercussions body image pressures can have on mental and physical health seriously. Similar laws to the aforementioned have been rolled out in France, Israel and Norway in a bid to safeguard people.

After all, leading UK eating disorder charity Beat states that issues with body image can result in an individual developing an eating disorder, although it is also careful to point out that such illnesses are generated by a range of things. Around 1.25 million individuals in the UK are estimated to have an eating disorder such as bulimia or anorexia nervosa or issues with binge eating, with the majority, but not all, being women.[251] Men are by no means immune to body image pressure, though. Research by suicide prevention charity Campaign against Living Miserably (CALM) found that nearly half of UK men said poor body image has had an impact on their mental health, while nearly six in ten young men felt unhappy with their bodies because of the Covid-19 crisis.[252]

A story of mine for *The Independent* revealed that demand for the charity Beat tripled during the pandemic, with the service experiencing record levels of people coming forward to seek help.[253] Experts at the time attributed this to an overall rise in anxiety combined with an increased emphasis on cooking and exercise during the Covid crisis, as well as people spending more time on social media. Teenage angst can provoke enough of an existential crisis, without also having to wrestle with the brutal popularity contest that is social media and the late-night doom scrolling that can be hard to resist. Irrespective of age, however, it is all too easy to forget that many of the bodies you look at in adverts have been photoshopped and airbrushed to look flawless.

THE STATS

> The Health Survey for England, which polled 8,205 adults in 2019, discovered that more than one in four young women have a potential eating disorder and around one in eight male adults has a possible eating disorder.[254]

> Young LGBTQ+ people are three times more likely to have previously had an eating disorder or to still be suffering from one, with girls who are lesbian or bisexual more than twice as likely as straight girls to have an eating disorder.[255]

> Anorexia has the highest mortality rate of all psychiatric illnesses.[256]

> Waiting times for services helping children with eating disorders have surged to record levels, and charities warn that this is placing children's lives at risk.[257]

> A report by MPs has warned that the government's stance on addressing eating disorders and poor body image is 'dangerous' and that health professionals' use of the body mass index must be axed now.[258]

> The same research, by the Women and Equalities Committee, found that the coronavirus crisis has had 'devastating' repercussions for people who have or are at high risk of eating disorders, as well as exacerbating body image anxieties.

> One in five adults felt shame, while around a third felt down or low, and almost two in ten felt disgusted, by their body image in the last year.[259]

> The same polling found that around a third of adults have felt anxious or depressed due to their body image, and one in eight adults had grappled with suicidal thoughts due to rumination about body image. [260]

> Around one in five adults said images employed in ads had made them worry about their body image, while four in ten teens said social media images had spawned body image concerns.[261]

> Six in ten consider the media to be pushing unachievable body image pressures for both genders, while eight in ten believe the fashion world has damaged views on appearance.[262]

> A study by the University of South Australia, which describes 'drunkorexia' as the 'damaging and dangerous' practice of cutting down on eating while drinking excess alcohol in a bid to stop putting on weight, found that over 80 per cent of female university students polled had done this in the previous three months.[263]

THE WINS

> The body positivity movement came to the fore as the fat acceptance movement in 1969. A young New York-based engineer called Bill Fabrey set up the National Association to Aid Fat Americans, which is now called the National Association to Advance Fat Acceptance.

> The Digitally Altered Body Image Bill was proposed in UK parliament in 2022, which would have necessitated advertisers and influencers to tag images that have been digitally altered, although the legislation did not succeed.

> The body positivity movement has exploded on Instagram in recent years.

> Research has found that seeing body-positive content on Instagram boosted young women's mood and feelings about their body in comparison to seeing 'thin-ideal' or 'appearance-neutral' posts on the social media platform.[264]

> Boots, John Lewis, Marks & Spencer, Boohoo, Dove, Barry M and PureGym signed an agreement not to digitally change body proportions in content, promotions or ads.

> Fashion and advertising have started to display more diverse bodies in recent years, using more plus-size or 'curve' models, although this does not apply to high fashion.

RESOURCES

> Changing Faces – leading UK charity supporting individuals with a scar, mark or condition on their body or face.

> The Body Happy Org – social enterprise seeking to improve children's body image.

> Body Positive Alliance – organisation campaigning for body equality and acceptance.

> Beat – UK's leading eating disorder charity which runs a helpline.

> National Association to Advance Fat Acceptance – long-running US organisation fighting for greater body positivity.

17

INTERSECTIONAL FEMINISM

'I am not free while any woman is unfree, even when her shackles are very different from my own.'

Audre Lorde

Who do you think has more power and agency over their lives: a woman of colour living in London working in a high-paid marketing job or an unemployed disabled white man living in Scarborough? I think I know who most people would pick when faced with this choice. Now I know this is something of a strange example, but please bear with me. It is this inequality that culture-war-stoking, bigoted politicians weaponise to erroneously claim that racism and gender inequality have been magically eradicated and that feminists who claim otherwise must quit their moaning. However, those who think like this are missing the point and are not taking an intersectional approach to matters of inequality.

Maya Angelou:

'EACH TIME A WOMAN STANDS UP FOR HERSELF, WITHOUT KNOWING IT POSSIBLY WITHOUT CLAIMING IT SHE STANDS UP FOR ALL WOMEN.'

While, yes, the Scarborough-based man is likely to have a tougher existence in many respects than the female Londoner, he will not have to endure the simultaneous racism, sexism and sexual harassment that the woman will experience. Moreover, this woman's individual success does not negate or do away with systemic and structural racism and misogyny. A quote by famous feminist author Roxane Gay springs to mind: 'Some women being empowered does not prove the patriarchy is dead. It proves that some of us are lucky.' The point is that inequalities do not exist in a vacuum. Instead, they coalesce, contradict and compound each other. This is where intersectional feminism comes into play. For those who have never heard of this term or are familiar with it but have never properly known what it means, intersectional feminism argues that race, gender, class, sexuality and ability must be examined together to understand inequality. This means that gender is not the only lens through which to consider inequality.

Kimberlé Crenshaw (see box), an Ohio-born lawyer, thought up the term intersectional feminism in 1989 in a bid to exemplify why Black women were unable to access legal redress for discrimination. Crenshaw noticed that Black women were being made to choose whether they were enduring racism or sexism when launching a workplace discrimination complaint; they could not pinpoint both. 'So, intersectionality was basically a metaphor to say they are facing race discrimination from one direction,' Crenshaw said in an interview about the case. 'They have gender discrimination from another direction, and they're colliding in their lives in ways we really don't anticipate and understand.'[265]

Describing the term on stage, Crenshaw explained: 'The way we imagine discrimination or disempowerment often is more complicated for people who are subjected to multiple forms of exclusion. The good news is that intersectionality provides us a way to see it.'[266] Nevertheless, the ideas that define intersectional feminism existed long before the term emerged. The role of black feminists in the 1970's cannot be overlooked when understanding its genesis. For me, intersectional feminism provides the perfect panacea to liberal feminism, white feminism, individualistic girl-boss feminism and carceral feminism. Those last four strands of feminism are schools of thought many unknowingly subscribe to despite perhaps never having heard of them.

The main issue with liberal feminism – which is centred around achieving gender equality via political and legal means – is that it is often based on a narrow, non-inclusive view of what it means to be a woman. White feminism can be criticised for the same reasons. Like a parent who is only interested in their own kids, liberal feminists tend to be less interested in issues that do not affect them, such as the women dragged into the criminal justice system for shoplifting to support their partner's drug addiction, or the women forced to sell sex because they don't make enough money to buy new school uniforms for their kids. Despite the gravity of these issues, to the average liberal feminist they appear to feel too tragically extreme and detached from their own life experiences to be a priority. Moreover, this disinterest will often extend to far less distressing examples than those given.

On the whole, the traditional liberal feminist is far more interested in campaigning for issues she herself can relate to – which feel relevant to her own life. The classic liberal feminist goals would be centred around getting more women into board rooms and more statues of high-profile women on city streets. Causes that feel as helpful to women in low-paid, precarious employment who are having to choose between heating and eating as a new café selling £15 plates of smashed avocado on toast, which you could easily whip up at home for a fraction of the price.

Increasing representation of women politicians would be a key goal of liberal and individualist feminism. And while representation is of course important – and I believe that the adage 'you can't be what you can't see' makes sense and it is key to have women in senior positions in all walks of life – it is not enough on its own. A woman politician implementing xenophobic policies and spouting bigoted rhetoric is hardly a win for gender equality. In the UK, getting more women in board rooms or in the upper echelons of the Conservative Party is unlikely to stop the disproportionate number of women in low-paid, unstable work who are crippled by the cost-of-living crisis. Let's not forget that women made up as much as 98 per cent of workers taking home poverty wages in high-coronavirus-exposure jobs in the first wave of the pandemic.[267]

But what about carceral feminism? This hinges on using systemically flawed institutions riddled with human rights abuses – namely prisons and policing – to solve gender inequality and sexual harassment and violence. It often feels like those who espouse carceral feminism are unaware of, or wilfully turn a blind eye to, the injustice of the criminal justice system. The term carceral feminism was first used by Elizabeth Bernstein, a professor of women's studies and sociology at Barnard College, Columbia University. She used the term in her 2007 article 'The Sexual Politics of the "New Abolitionism"'. Carceral feminism takes the scorched-earth, punitive and sometimes vengeful approach of 'lock 'em up and throw away the key' to male perpetrators of violence. Rather than focusing on preventative attempts to re-educate men on gender-based violence, it directs its efforts on being reactive. Taking an intersectional approach to inequality helps to counteract this reductive way of thinking.

Nevertheless, looking at the world from an intersectional perspective requires being able to hold multiple ideas in your head at the same time, grasping and respecting complexity, nuance and contradiction, while avoiding reductive, binary, black-and-white thinking. Without wanting to sound condescending or defeatist, I think it's an approach that some people find easier to get their head around than others. And it is arguably this – the contradictory, fluctuating nature of inequality – that leaves some unable to understand, engage with or relate to feminism.

INTERSECTIONAL FEMINISM

Gender inequality does not exist in a vacuum. On the contrary, it is inextricably linked to other forms of oppression, such as race, class, sexuality, disability, religion, immigration status and caste. At its simplest, intersectional feminism is about expanding feminism so it shines a light on intersecting forms of oppression rather than solely seeing the world through the lens of gender. The term 'intersectional feminism' was the brainchild of Kimberlé Crenshaw, an Ohio-born lawyer and prominent critical race theorist. Crenshaw conceived the term back in 1989 but until recently it was the reserve of academics. Now, however, it is far more mainstream. 'Intersectionality' officially landed in the *Oxford English Dictionary* in 2015, which defines it as: 'The interconnected nature of social categorisations such as race, class, and gender, regarded as creating overlapping and interdependent systems of discrimination or disadvantage; a theoretical approach based on such a premise.'

18

MENOPAUSE

'It's a time of liberation. It's a time of shedding the
shackles of inhibition and of giving a damn.'

Davina McCall

Women's bodies are idolised and commodified when they are
young, taut and scantily clad, but when talk turns to periods,
childbirth or the menopause, the zeal for women's bodies
dwindles. Society has long dismissed the menopause, and the
disinterest in and distaste for older women has meant that
this time of a woman's life is widely ignored or misunderstood. Though there are an estimated 13 million menopausal
women in the UK – a substantial chunk of whom will be experiencing debilitating and paralysing symptoms, ranging from
heart palpitations to hot flushes, from vaginal pain to changes
in mood – the menopause has been spectacularly absent from
public life and consciousness.[268] Throughout history, the menopause has been omitted from political discussions, workplaces,
medical training programmes and popular culture.

For a long time, the menopause only popped up in conversations when it was the butt of some wit-deficient joke about hot flushes. This is probably the most widely recognisable menopausal symptom, but it is just one of many. Symptoms of menopause include vaginal dryness, night sweats, insomnia, headaches, a reduced sex drive and recurrent urinary tract infections, as well as mood changes, feelings of sadness, difficulty concentrating and issues with memory.

In fact, it is often the mental health repercussions that health professionals say are the most disabling. At their starkest, these can see women quitting their jobs and withdrawing from their old lives, spending more time at home in their inner worlds, where they needlessly agonise over the past and fear the future. Previous exclusive research I covered from the Newson Health Menopause & Wellbeing Centre, the largest menopause clinic in the UK, found that nine in ten women going through the menopause experience mental health issues, with many suffering from anxiety and depression.[269]

This is one of the areas in this pocket guide where progress has been coming on in leaps and bounds in recent years. Discussion of the menopause now abounds on social media, in media coverage and among brands – the last of these must be approached with caution and necessitates a watchful, discerning eye. Increasing numbers of high-profile figures have spoken publicly about their own personal experiences of the menopause. Davina McCall has been at the forefront of this, with the veteran presenter fronting two Channel 4 documentaries about the menopause. In being so courageously honest about her struggles with hot flushes, depression and memory loss, McCall has helped to kill off some of the age-old stigmas that have enveloped this issue and impeded progress on tackling it.

But there is far more to be done, and even though we have seen significant change, menopausal women in the UK are still routinely denied the help they need and deserve. Research from the Menopause Support Network, shared exclusively with me for an article for *The Independent*, suggested that almost half of women going through the menopause say they were left with no option but to seek private healthcare.[270] Healthcare providers told me that menopausal women are resorting to private treatment after failing to get proper support or correct prescriptions from NHS doctors. Campaigners told me that some women are racking up debt by borrowing money from the bank or relatives, as private treatment can spiral into costing thousands of pounds.

Another major issue to contend with has been the ongoing hormone replacement therapy (HRT) shortage, which has left pharmacy shelves empty around the UK. For the record, HRT alleviates symptoms of the menopause. For many women, it is the difference between being able to lead a normal life and plunging to rock bottom – psychologically and physically. From being forced to substantially reduce their dosage to make it last longer, to ringing round dozens of pharmacies to find that no one has the product they need, menopausal women across the country have experienced anxiety, frustration and anguish because of this deficit. On top of this, despite HRT being free in Scotland and Wales, this is not the case in England. Meanwhile, a report by the All-Party Parliamentary Group on Menopause found that doctors still aren't giving many women the option of HRT.

It is not just that women often struggle to receive the correct menopause treatment, though; sometimes they are given the wrong treatment entirely. Depressingly enough, a previous poll by Channel 4 found that two-thirds of women were offered antidepressants for symptoms of the menopause despite there being no proof that antidepressants will relieve symptoms of the menopause; in some cases, it can even exacerbate them.[271]

In part, this is driven by GPs' ignorance about the menopause due to the dearth of training and education offered on this subject.

Issues surrounding the menopause are not unique to the UK. Many of the hundreds of millions of menopausal women around the world are also battling against similar problems. 'Unfortunately, both awareness and access to menopause-related information and services remain a significant challenge in most countries,' the World Health Organization (WHO) states. 'Menopause is often not discussed within families, communities, workplaces, or health care settings.' The WHO also warns that 'health-care providers may not be trained to recognise perimenopausal and post-menopausal symptoms', adding that the menopause presently gets 'limited attention in the training curricula for many health care workers'.[272]

To return to the UK, it can seem as though the awareness raised around the menopause has been more impactful than it has in reality. If you listen to BBC Radio 4's *Woman's Hour*, read the *Guardian*, watch Channel 4 and orbit a certain Instagram or Twitter sphere, you will have seen a growing discussion on the menopause, but other Britons will be far less aware of the so-called 'menopause revolution'. While there appears to be more awareness that working-class women in the UK may not be reaping the benefits of progress in understanding the menopause, there needs to be more work to tackle this. I would hazard a guess that there are still many menopausal women across the country suffering in silence as they wonder what on earth is happening to their mind, body and soul. This is likely to be especially true for transgender men assigned female at birth and non-binary people going through the menopause, who face additional stigma.

Improving support for those going through the menopause has ripple effects. You are not just helping their physical and mental health, you are helping their relationships with loved ones, the economy and humanity. It is also important for younger women to support the older women in their communities who are going through the menopause, and to elevate the conversation, for the benefit of all the women in our lives, but also for our future selves.

THE STATS

> The number of HRT prescriptions in England has doubled in the last five years, from January 2017 to December 2021.[273]

> HRT prescription rates are substantially lower in more deprived parts of England than in wealthier areas.[274]

> While suicide is a complex, multi-causal issue, some campaigners and health professionals suggest there could be a link between untreated menopause symptoms and suicide, with suicide rates for women being at their highest between the ages of 45 and 54 years.[275]

> Four in ten medical schools in the UK do not have mandatory menopause education on the curriculum.[276]

> The UK could be losing 14 million work days a year as a result of the menopause.[277]

> Lack of support in the workplace for women going through the menopause is driving female workers out of their jobs and prompting the UK economy to 'haemorrhage talent'.[278]

> One in ten women in the UK who worked while going through the menopause has left their job due to suffering menopausal symptoms.[279]

> A 2022 US study found that Black women go through the menopause at a younger age than white women and expe-

rience worse symptoms, yet they are less likely to take hormone therapy or access medical and mental health services – the researchers warn of structural racism.[280]

❯ Almost a quarter of women around the world are uncomfortable discussing the menopause.[281]

❯ Many governments have neither health policies nor funding for health treatment for the menopause as part of standard services.[282]

THE WINS

❯ Davina McCall fronted two widely watched, influential Channel 4 documentaries about the menopause in 2021 and 2022.

❯ Over 2,000 employers, including the BBC, AstraZeneca, Royal Mail, TSB and Co-op, have signed up to the Menopause Workplace Pledge, which involves providing support to menopausal employees.

❯ An All-Party Parliamentary Group (which includes MPs from a range of political parties) focused on the menopause was established in 2021. The group is chaired by Carolyn Harris, a Labour MP who has promised to bring in a 'menopause revolution'.

❯ The UK government reduced the cost of HRT in April 2023, allowing women to save £205 each year, but campaigners want ministers to go further and make HRT totally free as it is in Scotland and Wales.

❯ Assessments for future doctors will look at the menopause from 2024/25.

❭ In February 2023 Labour unveiled a policy pledge that would require large employers to release menopause action plans every year. Menopausal employees would potentially be given paid time off work and uniform changes.

RESOURCES

❭ The Menopause Charity – striving to raise awareness of the menopause.

❭ British Menopause Society – UK's authority for menopause and post-reproductive health.

❭ Newson Health Menopause & Wellbeing Centre – specialist perimenopause and menopause clinic.

❭ Black Girl's Guide to Surviving Menopause – a podcast and support network focused on the experiences of Black women, trans and gender diverse people.

❭ Menopause Café – a place for people to gather and discuss the menopause over cake and tea.

❭ Menopause Support – works with over 33,000 women supporting them through menopause, provides training for organisations and campaigns for greater education for menopause in doctors training and in schools.

'I think **TRANSWOMEN** and **TRANSPEOPLE** in general, show everyone that you can **DEFINE** what it means to be a **MAN** or **WOMAN** on your own terms.'

— **LAVERNE COX**

19

HONOUR-BASED ABUSE

'When we love rightly we know that the healthy,
loving response to cruelty and abuse is putting
ourselves out of harm's way.'

bell hooks

In the Cambridge Dictionary, honour is defined as 'a quality that combines respect, being proud, and honesty'. As such, honour is not a trait most would associate with murder, or covertly taking girls or women abroad to force them into marriages to strangers, or with coercive control, or female genital mutilation (FGM). However, these are all phenomena that fall under the remit of honour-based abuse. So-called honour-based abuse is different to most other crimes in the sense that it is perpetrated by the people in the world many of us hold nearest and dearest: family. Nevertheless, sometimes it transcends the family and is instead committed by the wider community. It is a complex crime, which can have numerous interconnected perpetrators.

Honour-based abuse is perpetrated with the aim of safeguarding a family's or a community's honour; those deemed to have tarnished their reputation feel their full wrath and are penalised accordingly. The notion of honour in this context eschews neat and tidy definitions, instead being a slippery, ambiguous and ultimately subjective idea. Although saying that, the honour being upheld here is often imbued with misogyny, homophobia and transphobia. For this reason and more, all manner of atrocities are committed in the name of honour. At its starkest and darkest, this involves murder. A while back, the United Nations estimated that some 5,000 'honour killings' occur around the world every single year.[283] However, experts deem there to be more killings than these numbers suggest.

Honour-based abuse manifests in a plethora of ways – in everything from assault, child marriage, virginity testing, and sexual violence to economic abuse, forced abortion, attempted murder, threats to kill and more. But what causes an individual to think that someone has besmirched their honour? Perhaps having a relationship which someone in the family does not approve of or being friends with people the family do not approve of. It may be that the victim has had sex before marriage or fallen pregnant by the wrong person. It could include having an abortion or initiating divorce proceedings. Though this gives you some idea, purported transgressions surpass this list, extending to anything deemed to be ill-judged in some way.

While honour-based abuse is an issue I've written about a lot, and I've interviewed many survivors as well as frontline workers and campaigners, it is not a topic that gets much media attention. This neglect, for me, feels rooted in racism and misogyny. Women's lives have been confined to the private sphere throughout so much of history and the legacy of this persists, which is even more true for women in minoritised communities.

Perhaps unsurprisingly, honour-based abuse is a crime obscured by its stigma. This means it can be difficult to track down the statistics that capture its prevalence. In some ways, reporting honour-based abuse to the police is even harder than coming forward about domestic abuse, as it can involve speaking out about multiple individuals. Often, it does not just involve extricating yourself from one person, but from an entire community, irreversibly ostracising and isolating yourself in the process. It is not just men who perpetrate honour-based abuse; although experts argue that they constitute the majority of perpetrators, sadly women are also guilty of this.

Unfortunately, misconceptions about honour-based abuse abound in public institutions, such as the police, social services, educational settings and even sometimes among health professionals. It is routinely misconstrued as being an issue that only impacts south Asian communities, whereas in reality it occurs in a range of communities. A study into honour-based abuse in the UK discovered that a dearth of proper data obfuscates the stark reality of the issue, while researchers also found reports of honour-based abuse in Eastern European and Middle Eastern communities.[284]

Do not be misguided by the term honour-based abuse, which arguably fails to adequately capture the horror of the phenomenon; this is a brutal issue. Virginity testing and FGM are among two of the most patently grim manifestations of honour-based abuse. FGM, internationally recognised as a human rights violation, refers to any procedure that intentionally alters female genital organs for non-medical reasons. The procedure is often carried out without anaesthesia and can cause a lifetime of severe health problems and pain. Experts and FGM survivors say sometimes the practice is inflicted to make sex less pleasurable and more painful in a bid to prevent women from having sex before marriage or from cheating on their partners. If you want an example of malignant misogyny, this is as good as any.

A study by two arms of the United Nations predicted that progress on stopping FGM would be profoundly impeded by the Covid-19 pandemic, as researchers tragically estimated that 2 million FGM cases may take place during the next 10 years that could be avoided.[285] There are more than 200 million girls and women who have endured FGM in 30 countries in the Middle East, Africa and Asia, according to the World Health Organization.[286]

Virginity testing, on the other hand, refers to highly intrusive and potentially traumatic vaginal examinations, to see if the hymen is intact. Unsurprisingly, they are deemed a serious infringement of human rights by the United Nations. The World Health Organization states that the practice is also a sham because the hymen can rip for a number of reasons, such as using a tampon or doing exercise.

Tellingly and worryingly, the UK Home Office has only had a compulsory obligation to gather data on honour-based abuse offences from police forces since April 2019. Karma Nirvana, which runs a national helpline as well as training the police, NHS and social services about forced marriage and honour-based abuse, state every year that they have seen an increase in reports to their national honour abuse helpline. Natasha Rattu, the charity's director, who I've interviewed many times, has long been fearful that thousands of honour-based crimes cease to ever be identified, meaning perpetrators can often operate with impunity.

Rattu also warns of a dearth of adequate training in dealing with honour-based abuse for police officers, social workers, health professionals and teachers. She notes that professionals can worry that they will be deemed racist, overly interfering or culturally insensitive if they take action on these crimes. Meanwhile, frontline workers tell me it is common for professionals to ask victims the wrong questions and to miss the signals. There are also said to be issues around the authorities being duped by relatives who deny they are perpetrating this kind of abuse – something Rattu once memorably referred to as 'Oscar-winning performances' by family members.[287]

So the question remains: why does honour-based abuse remain so overlooked and neglected in the UK? The role of systemic and structural racism and misogyny cannot be underestimated. For many working in this sector, and for the loved ones of individuals whose lives have been claimed by honour-based abuse after the authorities failed to take reports seriously, it can feel like the government and the police simply do not care enough about the victims.

THE STATS

> The number of honour-based abuse offences recorded by police forces in England has surged by 81 per cent, increasing from 884 in 2016 to 1,599 in 2020.[288]

> According to SafeLives, 54 per cent of domestic abuse victims at risk of enduring honour-based abuse were abused by numerous individuals.[289]

> Around 76 per cent of victims of honour-based abuse are estimated to be women by a Crown Prosecution Service report.[290]

> Karma Nirvana, a national charity supporting victims of honour-based abuse, saw a 57 per cent rise in calls during the Covid-19 lockdown, with frontline workers warning that honour-based abuse was exacerbated by the pandemic.[291]

> His Majesty's Inspectorate of Constabulary reported that a meagre 3 out of 43 police forces were 'well prepared for the complexity that honour-based violence can pose' after conducting the first national review into how honour-based abuse is policed in 2015.[292]

> Some 137,000 women and girls are living with the repercussions of FGM in the UK.[293]

> Official data released by UNICEF claims that FGM affects at least 200 million women around the world, but Equality Now, a non-government organisation that promotes the rights of women and girls, suggests this 'woefully' underestimates both the nature and scale of the issue.[294]

> There is growing evidence that FGM takes place across the world, in numerous countries in Europe, the Middle East, Africa, Asia, North America and Latin America.

> Some 5,000 honour killings are estimated to take place around the world every year, but this data is deemed to profoundly underestimate the scale of the problem.[295]

> Some 15,222 honour killings are estimated to have been recorded between 2004 and 2016 in Pakistan – 1,170 every year and 22 each week.[296]

THE WINS

> The Remember Heshu campaign, carried out by the Iranian and Kurdish Women's Rights Organisation (IKWRO) in 2002, called for the murder of a London-based British-Kurdish teen called Heshu Yunes by her father to be viewed as an 'honour' killing during a time when there was far less awareness of this issue.

> Laws making it illegal to force someone into marriage in England and Wales were implemented in 2014.

> In 2018, there were three defendants convicted in two separate cases for the specific offence of forced marriage – the first in England.

> Honour Abuse Research Matrix (HARM), a multi-disciplinary global research network bringing together academics, survivors, frontline workers, policy makers and others, was launched to tackle honour-based abuse.

> Legislation was passed in Pakistan in 2016 that stops individuals convicted of 'honour killings' of female relatives being pardoned by family members for blood money, resulting in killers receiving a mandatory life sentence and closing a loophole that permitted thousands of murderers to evade punishment.

> New legislation banning child marriage came into force in England and Wales in 2022. The legal age of marriage was raised to 18, meaning 16- and 17-year-olds can no longer get married or have a civil partnership, even if their parents give consent.

> So-called virginity tests and procedures claiming to repair the hymen were made illegal in England and Wales in 2022.

RESOURCES

> Karma Nirvana helpline – national charity supporting victims of honour-based abuse that runs a free helpline.

> Iranian and Kurdish Women's Rights Organisation (IKWRO) – UK charity which helps victims of honour-based abuse.

> Savera UK – charity striving to eradicate honour-based abuse.

> Halo Project – supports Black and minoritised survivors of honour-based abuse, forced marriage, FGM, domestic abuse and sexual violence.

> Honour Abuse Research Matrix (HARM) – research network.

20

TRANSPHOBIA

'They can try all they want to erase us, but at some point, they will realise the trans community is never going away.'

Charlotte Clymer

If I had to describe transphobia in three words, I would opt for: hateful, paranoid and obsessive. And if I had to pinpoint three causes of transphobia, I would opt for misandry (defined as the hatred of men), a crude, biologically deterministic view of the world, and unabated bigotry. For those who do not know what transgender means, the Cambridge Dictionary describes it as 'someone whose gender does not match the body they were born with'. Transphobia refers to a spurious fear, revulsion and hatred of the trans community, with the Merriam-Webster Dictionary defining the term as an 'irrational fear of, aversion to, or discrimination against transgender people'.

Transphobia can manifest itself in numerous ways, from politicians and campaigners attempting to clamp down on the rights of transgender people, to not providing proper health-care and using incendiary, bigoted rhetoric against trans people. The latter can range from overt transphobia to veiled dog whistles. But it is not just trans people who face discrimi-nation, non-binary and gender-diverse individuals also grapple with prejudice and bigotry. While the number of people in the UK who identify as transgender may be very small, the issue nevertheless continues to get a tonne of airtime in polit-ical debates and within the media. For the record, more than 250,000 people over the age of 16 in England and Wales iden-tify as transgender.[297] This is a minuscule proportion of the population when you consider that there are estimated to be over 67 million people in the UK.

Despite this, transphobia remains the most omnipresent, rampant and socially acceptable form of bigotry in the UK, with salacious transphobic articles lining newspaper pages, columns and social media news feeds. In great swathes of the tabloid press, the perceived appetite for transphobic news stories feels insatiable. IPSO, which is the UK's Indepen-dent Press Standards Organisation, documented a 400 per cent rise in the coverage of 'trans issues' by the mainstream media from 2009 to 2019.[298] Of course, transphobia does not just pervade public discourse; it also saturates public spaces. Moreover, the two issues are inextricably linked, providing an example of how violent rhetoric can have tangible real-world repercussions.

After all, abuse and violence towards transgender people is troublingly prevalent in the UK. Data from the Home Office revealed that hate crimes targeting transgender people surged by 56 per cent in England and Wales between the year ending March 2021 and the year ending March 2022 – rising from 2,799 to 4,355.[299] Across the Atlantic, in the so-called free world, the trans community has to grapple with sky-high poverty rates and politicians using their gender identity to ramp up the culture wars, and in some states they face legislatures launching direct attacks on their civil liberties, rights and freedoms. A clear example of the injustice they face can be seen in Trump's ban on trans people openly serving in the US military – a policy the new US president Joe Biden has fortunately reversed. Another is the legislation that Republican lawmakers in Florida passed in April 2023 that empowers the state to take children away from their parents when they are 'at risk' or 'subjected to' gender-affirming healthcare. Unsurprisingly, the legislation has been branded 'fascist' and criticised as 'state sponsored kidnapping' of trans kids.

In the UK, it is often said that we have some of the most virulently transphobic media coverage in the world. Here, much of the debate over trans rights has revolved around politicians and certain feminists seeking to ensure that trans women are unable to enter women's toilets. Those feminists who espouse this view are branded TERFs (short for trans-exclusionary radical feminists) or gender critical feminists.

Such individuals have repeatedly raised fears that predatory men will deliberately pretend they are trans women in a calculated effort to enter women-only areas. Toilets are often cited as a place where this could happen, despite the fact research has found there is no evidence that enabling trans people to use bathrooms tallying with their gender identity leads to a rise in dangerous incidents.[300] Moreover, the Equality Act, rolled out back in 2010, safeguards transgender people's rights to enter the single-sex spaces that tally with their self-determined gender. But this right is coming under increasing attacks from politicians and campaigners who disagree with this perspective. Rishi Sunak promised to overhaul the legal definition of sex during his bid to be Tory Party leader. Meanwhile, despite championing itself as the party of equality, the Labour Party remains bitterly divided about what egalitarianism looks like when it comes to trans rights and is home to a few gender critical feminists.

This brings me to a key difference between transphobia and other forms of bigotry, which it is important to emphasise: it is far, far more socially acceptable. Many warnings about letting trans women into women-only spaces are not just fearmongering and culture-war-stoking; they also invoke and unveil an implicit paranoia and suspicion that trans women are sexual predators or inherently dangerous, violent individuals. This is where my earlier reference to misandry comes from. Sometimes it feels like the hatred and mistrust of trans women is rooted in a refusal to see them as their self-determined gender and instead still view them as men. I understand how important it is to remember that some of the women who are deeply fearful of opening women-only spaces to trans women may have had traumatising experiences with men themselves – perhaps suffering domestic abuse and sexual violence in their lives. However, it is also important to see the real facts, which reinforce that trans women are not a threat to us.

Of course, it isn't just women who hold these transphobic views; there are also many men with such perspectives. The one unifying force that seems to ally transphobes is a deep, unshakeable fear of so-called biological sex or traditional gender constructs being disrupted.

Many of those who espouse transphobic views fervently will deny this is what they are doing, which can make it very difficult to engage in fruitful or constructive debates. Instead, their hatred of transgender people will sometimes be cleverly and carefully enveloped in an unconvincing veneer of political correctness – with diatribes against the trans community encased in purported declarations of support for trans rights, in turn confusing people and throwing them off guard. Nicola Sturgeon, who was formerly Scotland's first minister, had a point when she argued that some of those who oppose the gender-recognition reform she implemented in 2022 wield women's rights as a 'cloak of acceptability'.

It has always struck me as ironic that many feminists who oppose trans rights see themselves as being on the left, yet their view of humanity is at loggerheads with the well-established perspective of human nature espoused by left ideologies. A key dividing line between socialism and conservatism is the view each ideology takes to humanity. While socialism ultimately revolves around a positive view of people, conservatism posits humans are innately greedy and guided by self-interest. Being terrified of letting trans women into women's spaces suggests you ultimately have a negative view of humanity.

Another core tenet of transphobia involves questioning and ultimately denying the very existence of trans people. It is hard to know what lurks behind this, and it is no doubt a complex, multi-causal issue, but perhaps it is linked to egotism, as well as a lack of ability to empathise and show compassion. The mind of a transphobe may simply posit: 'I am not trans so nobody else can be.' Historical amnesia surrounding trans people and the lack of trans people in public life doesn't help matters. But it does feel like trans rights are under mounting attack as they become both cannon fodder and collateral damage in the culture wars. While there are many examples of this I could give you, here are just two. Take the fact that the Hungarian parliament voted by a landslide to get rid of teaching anything related to 'homosexuality and gender change' in public schools in 2021 – going so far as to erroneously, libellously affiliate LGBTQ+ rights with paedophilia. Or the fact that some areas have been declared trans-free in Poland.

Like other oppressed groups, trans people struggle to be heard. Supporting the trans community means fighting for human rights for all and dismantling patriarchal systems that crush both personal and societal growth. We are stronger together.

THE STATS

> Seven out of ten trans people say they have endured transphobia when seeking healthcare, while almost half of trans people and just over half of non-binary people say their GP failed to have a proper awareness of their needs.[301]

> One in four trans people does not tell any of their colleagues they are trans, while around two in five non-binary people say they are not out in the workplace.[302]

> Around two in five trans people have endured a hate crime or incident as a result of their gender identity in the last year.[303]

> LGBTQ+ individuals in more than half the world may not be legally safeguarded from being discriminated against through workplace legislation.[304]

> Most governments around the world refuse trans people the right to legally alter their name and gender from those they were assigned when they were born.[305]

> A quarter of the world's population thinks being LGBTQ+ should be a crime.[306]

> Homophobic and transphobic violence is linked with worse physical and mental health, such as a raised likelihood of anxiety, depression, self-harm and suicide.[307]

> Transgender women in the US are more likely to have lower cancer survival rates. Researchers have found that women who are sexual minorities are more likely to have no health insurance and to steer clear of healthcare because of its price.[308]

> There were 327 reported murders of trans and gender-diverse people from October 2021 to September 2022 – with most murders reported in the Caribbean and Latin America. Half of the murdered trans people whose job was documented were sex workers, while out of the cases that include details about race and ethnicity, Black and ethnic minority trans people constituted 65 per cent of murders.[309]

THE WINS

> The Supreme Court handed down a milestone LGBTQ+ rights decision ruling that discrimination against employees on the basis of sexual orientation or transgender status was against the law under the 1964 Civil Rights Act.

> Virginia Prince, a trans woman, set up *Transvestia* magazine in 1960, with some considering her a trailblazer in the movement for transgender rights.

> The Compton's Cafeteria riot exploded in San Francisco in August 1966, with trans people, drag queens and sex workers resisting harassment and violence from the police with high heels and bags, and a trans woman refusing arrest by hurling coffee at a police officer.

> Botswana's High Court rules a transgender man must be legally identified as a man in his official government documents in a milestone decision.

> Laverne Cox became the first transgender person to be on the cover of *Time* magazine in 2014.

> The Gender Recognition Reform Bill passed in Scotland in 2022 has made it easier for trans people to acquire a gender-recognition certificate, dropping the need for a medical diagnosis of gender dysphoria, as well as reducing the time a person would be required to live in their acquired gender from two years to three months.

> Over 1,600 scientists penned an open letter condemning the Trump administration's proposals to create a legal definition of gender that is set at birth in 2018.

RESOURCES

> Gendered Intelligence – charity supporting trans and gender-diverse people and raising awareness of gender diversity.

> Mermaids – one of the UK's most prominent LGBTQ+ charities that supports trans, non-binary and gender-diverse children, young people and families.

> Stonewall – UK's leading LGBTQ+ charity.

> Pink Therapy – directory of LGBTQ+-friendly counsellors and therapists.

> Transgender Law Center – biggest US national trans-led organisation campaigning for rights of trans and gender-diverse people.

> Stop Hate UK – charity delivering support to individuals impacted by hate crime running a free 24-hour reporting service.

> Stonewall Housing – UK's leading charity supporting LGBTQ+ people who are homeless or living in dangerous places.

21

CYBERSEX CRIMES

'Each time a woman stands up for herself,
without knowing it possibly, without claiming it,
she stands up for all women.'

Maya Angelou

What do spy-cam porn, upskirting, deepfake porn, cyber-flashing, sextortion and revenge porn all have in common? For one, they are all cybersex crimes. Secondly, they are all words that have only entered our vernacular in recent years.

Cybersex crimes are insidious, eerily perverse and, for the most part, committed by complete strangers through technology that is hard to trace. These crimes can involve installing hidden cameras in changing rooms, public toilets or tanning salons, snapping photos or recording videos up a stranger's skirt, as well as fiddling around on Photoshop doctoring images of celebrities to make them look like porn stars in explicit sexual positions, or sending unsolicited sexual images to strangers. And cybersex crimes aren't just committed by people you wouldn't recognise in the street; it is likely you would know the person who perpetrates so-called revenge porn (a phrase I do not like for reasons I will soon explain) against you.

While most of these repellent crimes might feel beyond the bounds of possibility for many, they nevertheless happen more often than many would assume. Let's start with revenge porn, as it is likely to be one of the most prevalent issues on the list of cybersex crimes – which, to be clear, is not comprehensive but covers six key issues in this shadowy, sinister realm. In its simplest terms, revenge porn involves revealing private sexual images or videos online or offline, without first gaining the consent of the person they concern, with the aim of provoking distress. Revenge porn was first made a criminal offence in the UK in 2015, with perpetrators facing prison sentences of up to two years. However, the law recently changed in 2021 to also punish those who threaten to share explicit private images or videos in the wake of the Naked Threat campaign launched by leading domestic abuse charity Refuge. Despite this progress, the number of people charged for revenge porn is dishearteningly low, with data showing that only 4 per cent of reports lead to court action, despite cases skyrocketing. Data obtained through Freedom of Information laws by Refuge show that 13,860 explicit-image crimes were recorded across 24 police forces from 1 January 2019 to 31 July 2022. However, a negligible 534 cases resulted in charges.[310]

Experts in the field object to the term revenge porn, instead preferring the decidedly clunkier, less memorable phrase 'intimate image-based abuse'. This is because the word 'revenge' implies the victim has done something to deserve having naked photos of them leaked to the world. In reality, revenge is just one of the manifold reasons perpetrators decide to leak explicit pictures or footage. Not that it is ever a fair or advisable form of reprisal. Take the BBC *Panorama* investigation which unearthed online groups with thousands of members known as 'subreddits' where men trade, sell and purchase personal photos of women. This phenomenon transcends Reddit and has been labelled 'collector culture'. 'So-called "collector culture" is a growing problem,' Zara Ward, who works in a senior role on the revenge porn helpline, told me. 'We see that these behaviours have evolved over time where the collectors will aim to avoid detection so content cannot be removed, and victims are left in the dark as to if their content has been shared illegally.'

It is worth bearing in mind there has been a considerable amount of legislation addressing cybersex crimes in recent years. Upskirting, defined as the act of covertly filming or taking a picture under a person's skirt without gaining their consent, was made a criminal offence in England and Wales in April 2019, while cyberflashing is also due to become a criminal offence in England and Wales. Further to this, the government has announced distributing deepfakes, explicit material manipulated to look like someone without their consent, will soon become illegal.

Sextortion is another growing issue in the UK and around the world. This involves explicit images or footage being used to blackmail an individual. The perpetrators are overwhelmingly organised crime contingents operating from abroad, but they can also be a partner or an ex. For those who no doubt find intimate image abuse and sextortion disturbing, then voyeurism will really unnerve you. For the blissfully unaware, voyeurism involves peeping toms installing clandestine cameras in rental and student properties or public spaces including toilets, swimming pool cubicles, changing rooms and tanning salons to capture explicit photos of women without their consent. This material is then uploaded to porn websites where, experts have informed me, there is a growing market for such material.

This is a growing problem in South Korea where the trend

termed 'spy-cam porn' is circulating online and is so wide-spread that it is sometimes referred to as an 'epidemic'. This is a crime predominantly perpetrated by men, and police in South Korea received more than 30,000 reports of covert cameras being used for filming between 2013 and 2018.[311] The country's lightning-fast internet permits images to be rapidly downloaded, distributed and sold. Human Rights Watch, a prominent global organisation, said the trend is having 'devastating' repercussions on victims, as the images can 'spread uncontrollably'.[312]

Online grooming is another grim cybersex crime that deserves attention. The Internet Watch Foundation states that girls are the victims in 92 per cent of all child abuse sexual content they remove from the internet.[313] The organisation considers online grooming to be a 'national crisis', warning that adult men have approached children as young as 11 online, with perpetrators duping young girls into taking off their clothes on livestreaming sites before the footage is distributed on child sex abuse sites. Adult offenders will pretend to be fellow teenagers or fake boyfriends, and experts warn that grooming can be done far more swiftly on the internet than in person. In essence, while sexual predators may be as old as the hills, the World Wide Web has offered perpetrators new and increasingly sophisticated ways to execute their sick and twisted exploits. Sadly, around the world, the criminal justice system has often been sluggish in staying on top of these issues, especially as the internet evolves and develops.

THE STATS

> Calls to the national Revenge Porn Helpline about threats to share intimate images more than tripled between 2017 and 2020.[314]

> A report by the Revenge Porn Helpline branded 'collector culture' – gathering, uploading and trading intimate material of women – as 'an emerging trend' that is 'increasing at pace'.

> A rugby group at Oxford Brookes University urged players to get as many nudes of women at the university as they could to disseminate and rate.

> A private Bristol Facebook group where men distribute explicit photos and videos of women, including content of their ex-partners, accumulates 7,000 members in days.

> A US study states that women and children make up the majority of the victims of sextortion, with researchers saying that in many sextortion cases the perpetrators did not even have the photos or footage they were using to control and exploit their victims.[315]

> Sextortion cases reported to the UK's Revenge Porn Helpline almost doubled within a year, becoming the biggest issue it grapples with for the first time in 2021.[316]

> Data shows that more than a third of revenge porn cases are dropped by victims despite a suspect being identified. Charities warn that a 'potentially bruising' criminal justice ordeal without assurance of anonymity and a dearth of trust in the police are partially behind this.[317]

> In 2014, naked images of high-profile actors, musicians, models and presenters were leaked on the website 4chan,

an image-sharing forum, in a hack linked to the Apple iCloud service. The list was predominantly made up of female stars, including Jennifer Lawrence, Rihanna, Kim Kardashian, Kate Upton, Selena Gomez, Cara Delevingne and many more.

RESOURCES

> Women's Aid and Refuge – two leading domestic abuse charities who advise on partner-related cyber-sex crimes.

> Suzy Lamplugh Trust – personal-safety charity which runs the free National Stalking Helpline (0808 802 0300).

> Revenge Porn Helpline – free service that supports adults coping with intimate-image abuse.

> Internet Watch Foundation – removes child abuse imagery from the internet.

> Cyber Civil Rights Initiative – leading US organisation serving thousands of victims around the world.

22

FEMINIST ICONS TO GALVANISE YOU

While not all the women in this chapter explicitly label themselves feminists, if we look at their actions alongside the Cambridge Dictionary's definition of feminism, it seems reasonable enough to christen them all with this moniker. The Cambridge Dictionary defines feminism as 'the belief that women should be allowed the same rights, power, and opportunities as men and be treated in the same way, or the set of activities intended to achieve this state'.

MAYA ANGELOU

Who? Maya Angelou's life was so full and varied it almost feels like the author had stunt doubles filling in for her. Polymath is an overused word but one which this author, poet, composer, actor, dancer, singer, director, TV writer, journalist and civil rights activist truly deserves. Also a memoirist, Angelou's multiple works of autobiographical writing explore her experiences and observations of racial segregation, injustice and racism growing up in the Deep South.

What? Angelou is probably best known for *I Know Why the Caged Bird Sings*, her first autobiographical piece of writing about her childhood in the 1930s which was published in 1970. The book won her a National Book Award nomination and was turned into a film. Angelou's life was coloured by a series of firsts and prestigious accolades. To name just a few, she was one of the first African American women to have a screenplay turned into a feature film. Moreover, she won Grammys for her spoken poetry and was nominated for a Pulitzer for her poetry. But there was more to Angelou than her words; she was also a talented dancer and singer, performing across the world in the 1950s.

Why? Always nuanced, never dogmatic, Angelou's prose is littered with wise insights and observations of inner and exterior worlds. In her own words: 'My mission in life is not merely to survive, but to thrive; and to do so with some passion, some compassion, some humour, and some style.' As well as exploring racial injustice, Angelou's writing also examines sexual violence through her own personal experiences and beyond. Angelou was raped by her mother's boyfriend at the age of seven on a trip to St Louis in Missouri. In turn, her rapist was imprisoned and swiftly murdered upon his release. He was thought to have been killed by her mother's brothers. Traumatised by the ordeal, Angelou did not speak for half a decade afterwards.

When? Born in St Louis in 1928 as Marguerite Ann Johnson, Angelou came to be known as Maya after her brother Bailey would say 'My-a sister'. As a young girl, Angelou was sent to live with her paternal grandmother in Stamps, Arkansas, as a result of her parents' volatile relationship. At just 16, Angelou gave birth to her first and only child Clyde 'Guy' Johnson.

Around this time, she worked as a cook, before going on to move to Los Angeles where she worked as a cocktail waitress.

How? Angelou's dogged determination was clear from a young age. She became the first African American woman to be a streetcar conductor in San Francisco as a teenager after initially being rejected for the position due to her race. While Angelou might have lost the power of words as a young girl, she sure made up for it afterwards. She joined the New York-based Harlem Writers Guild in 1959, an iconic collective made up of Black writers. Angelou's activism saw her collaborate with Martin Luther King and Malcolm X.

EMMA GOLDMAN

Who? Force of nature is neither a hyperbolic nor overblown title to give to Goldman. The activist and writer, who is probably one of the most famous anarchists in history, was steadfastly committed to pushing causes like freedom of expression, women's equality, sexual freedom, birth control and workers' rights, while simultaneously pushing back against military conscription, inequality, anti-worker laws, police violence and the broader oppression and exploitation of workers.

What? The mantra 'well-behaved women rarely make history' that has made its way onto a litany of tote bags, Instagram posts and keyrings can often be deployed too liberally. However, for Goldman, it rings true. The theorist had her fair share of run-ins with the law, with Goldman often finding herself arrested and sometimes behind bars. The Russian-born orator was frequently harassed or arrested while she was delivering speeches. Goldman, who was even blocked from giving speeches at times, was sentenced to a year in jail as she was deemed to have provoked a riot in New York which erupted after she gave a speech to unemployed women protesting in Union Square in 1893. 'If they do not give you work, demand bread. If they deny you both, take bread,' Goldman told the audience.

Why? Goldman, who wrote many books and essays, was passionate about individual freedom and autonomy but also the need for people to take collective action to create a new way of living. She saw abject poverty and injustice New Yorkers grappled with first-hand, working in textile factories and as a midwife. Goldman, a friend of Irish poet and playwright Oscar Wilde, was one of scant individuals who publicly condemned Wilde's conviction for homosexuality.

When? Born into a Jewish family in the Lithuanian city of Kaunas in 1869 during the Russian Empire, Goldman not only observed the abuse of peasants and brutal antisemitism but also appeared to have witnessed violence closer to home. In her book *Living My Life*, she recounts how she endured violent beatings from her father and her uncle. Goldman, who became a British citizen in her later years, went on to flee an arranged marriage, moving to the US at the age of 16.

How? Goldman's tactics ranged from delivering speeches to protesting, picketing and writing. In 1916, Goldman saw herself convicted for infringing New York legislation blocking lectures on birth control as it was not then legal. This culminated in something of a cat-and-mouse chase with the authorities, with Goldman paying a fine but carrying on giving speeches on birth control. She was then arrested again and sentenced to 15 days in prison after Goldman dismissed requests to fork out for another fine. A year later, she was arrested by J. Edgar Hoover, who went on to be the head of the FBI, for demonstrating against the First World War. Hoover branded Goldman 'one of the most dangerous women in America' and had her deported even though she was a US citizen. In her own words: 'Can there be anything more outrageous than the idea that a healthy, grown woman, full of life and passion, must deny nature's demand, must subdue her most intense craving, undermine her health and break her spirit, must stunt her vision, abstain from the depth and glory of sex experience until a "good" man comes along to take her unto himself as a wife?'

REBECCA GOMPERTS

Who? Rebecca Gomperts might be something of a star in the global abortion rights movement, but she forever exudes modesty and humility. The Dutch doctor has spent her life helping women safely terminate pregnancies in nations where it is illegal, providing free or cheap abortions wherever and however she can. To do so, Gomperts has craftily circumvented legal loopholes, flown drones into locations filled with abortion pills, and sailed the seven seas to distribute safe medical abortions in international waters. The Portuguese government once ordered two warships to block her from sailing into their waters.

What? Since founding Women on Waves, a non-profit organisation of doctors and activists, back in 1999, Gomperts's tactics to provide abortions to those in desperate situations have constantly evolved. She set up Women on Web, a website and mail service which delivers abortion pills to women worldwide. More recently, in 2018, Gomperts launched Aid Access, which enables US-based women to obtain abortions and provides one of the cheapest ways to access abortion there.

Why? Gomperts is steadfast in her belief abortion is a human right and must be a safe, free, legal form of healthcare. Since the overturning of *Roe vs Wade* in the US, Aid Access is one of few services which provide medical abortions, doing so in nearly two dozen US states.

When? Born in 1966 in Suriname, a country on the north-eastern Atlantic coast of South America and a former Dutch colony, Gomperts moved to the Netherlands at the age of three. It was during a trip to Guinea where the seeds for her life's work appear to have been sown. Gomperts witnessed first-hand the unspeakable tragedy which can ensue after backstreet, clandestine abortions during her time there as she provided healthcare to women and watched some bleed to death before her eyes.

How? Gomperts is equal parts resourceful, versatile and imaginative. The doctor has a long inventory of tactics at her disposal, a prime example being the time she sued Trump health department secretary Alex Azar after the US Food and Drug Administration sent her a cease-and-desist letter, which she paid no notice to. This was then followed by Azar blocking payments to Aid Access and seizing abortion drugs she was prescribing in the post.

MARSHA P. JOHNSON

Who? Adorned in fur coats, sequins, Christmas lights, glittering chokers, flower headpieces and her signature smile – with many of her sparkling outfits gleaned from bins – Marsha P.

Johnson was as glamorous as she was gallant. A leading light in the New York gay rights movement of the 1960s and '70s, Johnson was part of the seismic 1969 Stonewall uprising, and she was only in her early twenties at the time. The uprising involved three nights of dissent after New York police raided a gay club in Greenwich Village called Stonewall Inn in the early hours. This uprising came in the context of a lengthy history of police brutality, harassment and homophobia. This riot is deemed to have provided the genesis for the broader gay rights movement, as well as serving as inspiration for Pride.

What? Johnson, a drag queen who was a core element of the Gay Liberation Front, championed the causes of LGBTQ+ young people who were homeless, individuals with HIV or AIDS, as well as transgender rights. Johnson herself was diagnosed with HIV in 1990. The activist ultimately helped the most marginalised communities, also campaigning on behalf of sex workers and prisoners.

Why? Johnson's zeal to fight for those most marginalised in society no doubt came from a place of empathy, compassion and understanding. The activist often found herself homeless and turning to sex work due to struggles to find work in a homophobic, transphobic climate where anti-LGBTQ+ sentiment was rife. While doing sex work, Johnson found herself facing violence and abuse from customers and then state-sanctioned abuse from the police who would arrest her. Clients are said to have pulled out guns on her and on one occasion the activist was shot.

When? Born in Elizabeth, New Jersey, in 1945, it didn't take long for Johnson to get to her spiritual home, with the activist moving to New York City's Greenwich Village after finishing high school in 1963. According to Johnson all she took with her was a bag of clothes and $15. It was upon arrival in New York that she changed her name to Marsha P. Johnson. The P. is said to stand for the phrase 'Pay It No Mind' which was often Johnson's rebuttal to those who interrogated her about her gender. Johnson died in 1992 at the age of just 46. Her body was discovered in New York's Hudson river in 1992 and the cause of her death is not known. A substantial proportion of those who were close to Johnson believe she was murdered, with an investigation into her death reopened in 2012, but still not solved.

How? Johnson has only gained proper acknowledgement for her activism posthumously. She helped set up Street Transvestite Action Revolutionaries (STAR), an organisation housing homeless LGBTQ+ young people which was the first of its kind. In her own words, 'I was no one, nobody, from nowheresville, until I became a drag queen.'

EMILY WILDING DAVISON

Who? Emily Wilding Davison was no stranger to arrests, stints in prison or hunger strikes. The suffragette, who campaigned for the right for women to vote, is probably most famous for her death which was captured in historic footage that continues to be played to this very day. Davison hurled herself in front of King George V's horse Anmer who was galloping at full speed at the Epsom Derby on 4 June 1913. Anmer seemingly emerged unscathed and finished the race but Davison lost consciousness and tragically died four days later in Epsom Cottage Hospital. Davison, who was a member of the Women's Social and Political Union (WSPU), was routinely arrested for her militant direct action. She was arrested nine times and went on hunger strike seven times.

What? While Davison was operated on, she ceased to recover, enduring internal injuries and a fractured scull and never recovering consciousness. After Davison's death, an inquest reached the conclusion of misadventure instead of suicide. But historians have debated Davison's exact motivations that fateful day – with some arguing she was attempting to pin a suffragette flag to King George V's horse. Two flags were discovered on Davison's body, according to police reports. Certain historians have argued Davison's dramatic deed could not have been a suicide attempt given she had a return train ticket from Epsom on her.

Why? Davison's activism was centred around militancy – with this including everything from arson, to assault, vandalism, sabotage, bombings and obstruction. As such, the suffragette spent a substantial amount of time in prison. Behind bars, her militancy showed no sign of abating, with Davison staging frequent hunger strikes, routinely being force-fed, barricading herself into the cell, and experiencing solitary confinement.

An official medical report on Davison after she tried to kill herself in the now-closed Holloway prison in north London in 1912 states: 'Obdurate, difficult temperament, at odds with society … a haggard appearance. Bruised in body and soul. Impulsively inclined and might do any rash act.'

When? Born in Greenwich in south-east London in 1872, Davison had two first-class university degrees yet was never formally awarded them as women were not permitted to graduate during those days. The suffragette, also a champion swimmer, had been and force-fed 49 times before she came head to head with King George V's horse.

How? Davison's zeal to get women the vote was reflected in her militancy, with Davison setting fire to postboxes, and smashing windows. 'Ours is a bloodless revolution but a determined one' Davison wrote to Herbert Gladstone, the then home secretary. Rather prophetically in hindsight, she told him herself and others were 'ready to suffer, to die if need be, but we demand justice'!

CONCLUSION

It is imperative that we do not forget just how recently many of women's hard-earned rights were introduced, and just how quickly powers and freedoms that took decades to fight for can be ripped away. Only a few decades ago, women in the UK could only access the contraceptive pill if they were married. This was effectively the state's way of saying you shouldn't be having sex outside of marriage. Although the contraceptive pill became available in 1961, at first it was exclusively for married women, only becoming more easily accessible via the NHS Family Planning Act in 1967.

What's more, let's not forget that marital rape only recently became illegal in the UK. Back in 1822, barrister John Frederick Archbold wrote that a husband 'cannot be guilty of a rape upon his wife'. However, a milestone court judgement changed this in 1991, with the House of Lords positing: 'Nowadays it cannot seriously be maintained that by marriage a wife submits herself irrevocably to sexual intercourse in all circumstances.' Nevertheless, it was not until 2003 that the illegality of marital rape was expressly outlined via the Sexual Offences Act.

Another disconcertingly recent example of misogyny is the existence of 'mother and baby homes' in Ireland, which removed tens of thousands of unmarried mothers and their babies from society for the majority of the twentieth century.

The institutions forced mothers and children to live in barbaric, abusive conditions, with some remaining open as recently as the early 1990s. Women living in such institutions have provided distressing evidence that they were not just forced into relinquishing their babies for adoption, but also forcibly incarcerated, and not remunerated for the labour they were made to carry out. And the crime that these women committed? Falling pregnant out of wedlock. While the majority of the homes were run by the Catholic Church, some were overseen by the state and a scant proportion were run by the Protestant Church.

Bearing in mind how recent these examples above were, it is no surprise that misogyny lingers on in society. While life has profoundly improved and progressed for women in the years since, historic and deeply ingrained prejudice, bigotry and injustice do not miraculously vanish overnight – something which those who downplay or altogether deny misogyny implicitly, and wrongly, suggest. In doing so, they invalidate centuries of suffering in a way that feels deludedly idealistic. Another shared habit of misogyny deniers is an obsession with pitting men and women against each other before promptly coming to the conclusion that it is actually men who are far worse off than women.

Someone who espouses such a view will often point to the fact that men are far more likely to be killed and injured in wars than women, as well as being more likely to be killed in gang violence. Yes, this is unequivocally true; yes, this is unequivocally tragic and yes, this does highlight the strain of being a man. But this perspective overlooks that it is generally men who are instigating the wars and initiating the gang violence, as well as enacting the policies that bar women from taking up military roles. What's more, it neglects how experts routinely warn that women and children are hardest hit by wars and humanitarian crises, and also that women are radically more likely to be subjected to sexual violence, domestic abuse and honour-based abuse. More importantly, though, comparing the plight of different demographics in an attempt to say that one group has it worse than the other is a futile, juvenile and dangerous exercise.

The views of misogynists are often imbued with misreadings and miscalculations. If an acquaintance or loved one started accusing you of stuff that made no sense and had no empirical basis, it is likely you would explain this to them rather than seriously engage with the nonsense they were spouting. It is tempting to take a similar approach to the manifold misconceptions that pervade feminism. Many of these fallacies are so ludicrous – feminists hate all men, feminists don't wear bras, feminists just need to get laid – they do not feel worthy of a rebuke. But rather than hastily dismiss misunderstandings of feminism or flippantly brush misreadings under the proverbial carpet, they must be confronted. That doesn't mean spending your days replying to every loser troll who spouts rubbish at you online, but it is worth correcting those misinformed friends or cultural-war-stoking politicians who twist and warp the meaning of feminism. This certainly shouldn't dominate your whole political *raison d'être*, but it should nevertheless form a part of it.

Sadly, there are many people out there who seem to think that being a feminist is akin to being a misandrist – defined as 'a person who dislikes, despises, or is strongly prejudiced against men' by the very useful dictionary in my laptop. And that probably isn't helped by the women, and men, who declare that all men are awful. There do seem to be a fair few people who make unhelpful sweeping statements of this kind – many of whom probably don't even believe what they are saying but just misguidedly consider it the trendy, politically correct thing to do. In my experience, those who parrot such assertions are in the minority.

During my encounters with such people, it often materialises that they have had genuinely horrific, and sometimes scary, experiences with men, and so they subsequently write off a whole gender. Throughout life you will meet people whose attitude to a certain gender or race of people will be unfairly based on the narrow experiences of their own lives, and this is a hard phenomenon to eradicate. There is certainly no shortage of men in the world who dismiss and despise all women – in fact, I've personally come across more men who do this than women.

Some men don't like feminism because they misperceive it as only helping women. In reality, it is about helping everyone – men included. Feminism's premise is simple. It is about wanting society to be a less bitterly unequal and cruel place. It is about not wanting to live in a country where rape has been effectively decriminalised, where between two and three women are murdered by their current or ex-partners every single week, and where police forces are plagued by scandal after scandal involving violent and sexually predatory officers.

One of the biggest misconceptions of feminism, and sometimes just of the left in general, is the notion that because you are critiquing society as it is, you are subsequently being ungrateful, negative and excessively pessimistic. When arguing with someone who takes such a view, your words can feel like they have been robbed from you and twisted into something altogether different. Seeing the reality around you with clear eyes, rather than through rose-tinted glasses, and calling out injustice, does not mean you are saying everything is awful. Yet that is the mad leap that naysayers of feminism and gender and racial equality will routinely make. They will reconfigure your words and admonish you for a point you haven't made.

'You're so negative,' they will say, perhaps after you have just said something critical about slavery or colonialism or the peculiar little island that is the UK. Quickly afterwards, you will notice them start performing mental gymnastics to misconstrue your arguments, and therefore impeding fruitful discussion and progress. Sometimes when you debate certain men who hate gender equality – whether that is a direct conflict on the internet, or you are just watching them emit their hateful views from a safe distance – it can feel as if you are arguing with a Machiavellian villain. In other words, it can seem like you are talking to someone who is wilfully ignoring you, distorting your words and being antagonistic. Perhaps the antagonist is not doing this deliberately, but their tactics feel underhand, covert and cunning.

Misogyny is all around us in the UK and across the world, like the smell of manure when you are standing slap bang in the middle of a farm. Despite this, many remain unable to get a whiff of misogyny's stench. In the same way that someone who suffers from anosmia (a condition that involves the loss of smell) would not be able to smell that manure in the middle of a farm, those who refute misogyny's existence remain blind to its omnipresence. Nevertheless, just as some with anosmia experience a partial loss of smell while others can't smell at all, the inability to recognise misogyny also exists on a spectrum. Moreover, just as most people experience anosmia fleetingly and temporarily as a consequence of developing a cold or Covid-19, so you would hope that most people who hold misogynistic views do not hold them dear forever.

Given that misogyny often stems from ignorance, I hope readers who were sceptical about misogyny and the continuing power of the patriarchy may have reassessed their perspective upon learning more. I also hope that those who felt unconfident about how the machinations of misogyny and patriarchy play out now feel more knowledgeable and better tooled-up to fight the systems of injustice.

ACKNOWLEDGEMENTS

Thank you to all the knowledgeable and dedicated individuals I have worked with over the years as a journalist. But also a special thank you to Chloe Hubbard, *The Independent*'s deputy editor, for creating the role of Women's Correspondent in the summer of 2018 after I suggested the job position and title. Also many thanks to my agent Rachel Mills, not only for invaluable support on this book, but for thinking *The Pocket Guide to Patriarchy* was a project worth pursuing after I proposed the idea. And last but not least, thank you to everyone at Orion Publishing for making this book come to life – with an extra special thank you to my publisher, Katie Packer, and my project editor, Frances Rooney.

ENDNOTES

INTRODUCTION

1 https://news.npcc.police.uk/releases/domestic-homicides-show-no-significant-increase-during-lockdown-says-new-police-report
2 https://www.thetrace.org/2016/02/women-domestic-violence-death-statistics/
3 https://www.unwomen.org/en/news/in-focus/commission-on-the-status-of-women-2012/facts-and-figures
4 https://www.ohchr.org/en/stories/2022/07/climate-change-exacerbates-violence-against-women-and-girls
5 https://www.guttmacher.org/report/abortion-worldwide-2017
6 https://www.who.int/news-room/fact-sheets/detail/abortion
7 https://www.who.int/health-topics/violence-against-women
8 https://www.who.int/news-room/fact-sheets/detail/violence-against-women
9 https://www.wfpusa.org/women-are-hungrier-infographic
10 https://wir2022.wid.world/chapter-1/

CHAPTER ONE

11 www.independent.co.uk/news/uk/home-news/anti-abortion-activism-uk-roe-wade-b2123460.html
12 https://www.bpas.org/media/3751/2020-aug-bpas-police-powers-unit-response.pdf
13 https://www.msichoices.org/news-and-insights/news/2020/2/9-in-10-uk-adults-now-identify-as-pro-choice/
14 https://www.unfpa.org/press/nearly-half-all-pregnancies-are-unintended-global-crisis-says-new-unfpa-report
15 https://www.guttmacher.org/article/2022/02/medication-abortion-now-accounts-more-half-all-us-abortions
16 https://www.independent.co.uk/news/uk/home-news/abortion-ministers-voting-records-b2219409.html
17 https://www.independent.co.uk/news/uk/home-news/what-is-having-abortion-like-b2018502.html

18 https://www.axios.com/2021/12/12/abortion-pills-access-ban-roe-wade-supreme-court

19 https://www.independent.co.uk/news/world/politics/pronatalist-countries-women-children-b1966249.html, https://populationmatters.org/disturbing-rise-in-countries-coercing-women-into-having-more-children-report-finds/

20 https://www.independent.co.uk/news/uk/home-news/abortion-uk-services-women-b2140656.html

21 https://www.independent.co.uk/news/uk/home-news/abortion-ministers-voting-records-b2219409.html

22 https://www.independent.co.uk/news/health/early-abortions-at-home-coronavirus-b1804276.html, https://www.fsrh.org/news/fsrh-statement-new-study-telemedicine-abortion-2021/

23 https://www.independent.co.uk/news/uk/home-news/abortion-women-police-investigation-rise-b2147009.html

24 https://www.guttmacher.org/fact-sheet/induced-abortion-worldwide

25 Ibid.

26 https://www.doctorswithoutborders.org/latest/unsafe-abortion-forgotten-emergency

27 Ibid.

28 https://reproductiverights.org/sites/default/files/documents/World-Abortion-Map.pdf

29 Ibid.

CHAPTER TWO

30 https://www.ons.gov.uk/peoplepopulationandcommunity/crimeandjustice/articles/improvingvictimisationestimatesderivedfromthecrimesurveyforenglandandwales/2019-01-24

31 https://www.femicidecensus.org/wp-content/uploads/2020/02/Femicide-Census-Report-on-2018-Femicides-.pdf

32 https://refuge.org.uk/what-is-domestic-abuse/the-facts/

33 *In Control*: Dangerous Relationships and How They End in Murder, Jane Monckton

34 https://www.independent.co.uk/news/uk/home-news/domestic-abuse-violence-assault-refuge-cuts-austerity-women-coercion-a9122006.html

35 https://news.npcc.police.uk/releases/domestic-homicides-show-no-significant-increase-during-lockdown-says-new-police-report

36 https://refuge.org.uk/what-is-domestic-abuse/the-facts/

37 ttps://www.justiceinspectorates.gov.uk/hmicfrs/wp-content/uploads/increasingly-everyones-business-domestic-abuse-progress-report.pdf

38 https://www.womensaid.org.uk/information-support/what-is-domestic-abuse/coercive-control/

39 https://www.independent.co.uk/news/uk/home-news/domestic-abuse-women-disabilities-helpline-b1850136.html

40 https://www.ons.gov.uk/peoplepopulationandcommunity/crimeandjustice/articles/domesticabusevictimservicesenglandandwales/november2021, https://www.birmingham.ac.uk/news-archive/2020/mortality-from-all-causes-over-40-per-cent-higher-in-female-domestic-abuse-survivors-1

41 https://www.independent.co.uk/news/uk/home-news/women-domestic-abuse-death-age-disease-cause-nhs-a9338831.html
42 https://www.independent.co.uk/news/uk/home-news/domestic-abuse-sexual-violence-transgender-nonbinary-people-b2257405.html
43 https://www.thetimes.co.uk/article/one-in-five-women-killed-by-their-partners-had-contacted-the-police-nc009nggl

CHAPTER THREE

44 https://www.bmj.com/content/368/bmj.m536.full
45 https://journals.plos.org/plosone/article?id=10.1371/journal.pone.0208260
46 https://www.huffingtonpost.co.uk/2015/09/03/women-spend-thousands-on-periods-tampon-tax_n_8082526.html
47 https://plan-uk.org/media-centre/over-one-million-girls-in-the-uk-struggled-to-afford-or-access-period-products-during-the-pandemic
48 https://www.wateraid.org/media/dirty-water-and-lack-of-safe-toilets-among-top-five-killers-of-women-worldwide
49 https://bmcwomenshealth.biomedcentral.com/articles/10.1186/s12905-020-01149-5
50 https://www.independent.co.uk/news/uk/home-news/periods-myths-menstruation-stigma-countries-b1852998.html
51 https://www.unicef.org/press-releases/fast-facts-nine-things-you-didnt-know-about-menstruation
52 https://www.ncbi.nlm.nih.gov/pmc/articles/PMC10014781/
53 https://www.independent.co.uk/news/uk/home-news/period-poverty-women-miss-school-work-office-money-sexism-a8786146.html
54 https://plan-uk.org/media-centre/over-one-million-girls-in-the-uk-struggled-to-afford-or-access-period-products-during-the-pandemic
55 https://plan-uk.org/media-centre/one-in-five-uk-girls-teased-or-bullied-because-of-their-period-new-survey-finds
56 https://www.worldbank.org/en/topic/water/brief/menstrual-health-and-hygiene
57 https://www.wateraid.org/uk/media/jacqueline-wilson-and-jodie-whittaker-join-wateraid-to-help-bust-period-taboos

CHAPTER FOUR

58 https://www.independent.co.uk/news/uk/home-news/gender-pay-gap-statistics-2022-equal-pay-day-b2216070.html
59 https://hbr.org/2018/06/research-women-ask-for-raises-as-often-as-men-but-are-less-likely-to-get-them
60 https://www.strategyand.pwc.com/uk/en/reports/ethnicity-pay-gap-report.pdf, https://www.independent.co.uk/business/gender-pay-gap-widest-for-women-in-their-50s-b2238840.html
61 https://www.independent.co.uk/news/uk/home-news/gender-pay-gap-uk-reporting-laws-countries-b1012831.html
62 https://www.theguardian.com/education/2021/aug/13/girls-overtake-boys-in-a-level-and-gcse-maths-so-are-they-smarter

63 https://news.sky.com/story/glacially-slow-progress-on-gender-equality-as-96-of-ceos-of-britains-largest-public-companies-are-men-12711481
64 https://papers.ssrn.com/sol3/papers.cfm?abstract_id=3617953, https://www.mckinsey.com/featured-insights/diversity-and-inclusion/diversity-wins-how-inclusion-matters
65 https://www.ons.gov.uk/employmentandlabourmarket/peoplenotinwork/economicinactivity/datasets/economicinactivitybyreasonseasonallyadjusted inac01sa
66 https://www.independent.co.uk/life-style/health-and-families/gender-pay-gap-government-east-of-england-east-midlands-alan-jones-b2287837.html
67 https://digital.nhs.uk/data-and-information/publications/statistical/personal-social-services-staff-of-social-services-departments/england-2019/individual-worker-characteristics, https://commonslibrary.parliament.uk/research-briefings/cbp-7756/
68 https://www.independent.co.uk/news/uk/home-news/women-unpaid-care-labour-b2319132.html
69 https://www.unicef.org/turkiye/en/node/2311
70 https://www.fawcettsociety.org.uk/news/fawcetts-2022-sex-and-power-index-reveals-that-less-than-13-of-uks-top-jobs-are-filled-by-women
71 https://www.lse.ac.uk/News/Latest-news-from-LSE/2021/c-March-21/Black-women-are-least-likely-to-be-among-UKs-top-earners
72 https://news-archive.exeter.ac.uk/research/2020/articles/covid-19adriverof-widespre.html
73 https://www.pewresearch.org/short-reads/2023/03/01/gender-pay-gap-facts/
74 https://www.actionaid.org.uk/our-work/womens-economic-rights/gender-pay-gap
75 https://www.bmj.com/content/374/bmj.n1972

CHAPTER FIVE

76 https://www.adl.org/resources/report/when-women-are-enemy-intersection-misogyny-and-white-supremacy
77 https://www.youtube.com/watch?v=_PS4R1JuVU4
78 https://counterhate.com/blog/youtube-rakes-in-millions-in-ad-revenue-from-videos-of-misogynist-andrew-tate/
79 https://ccis.ucsd.edu/_files/wp6.pdf
80 Ibid.
81 Ibid.
82 Ibid.

CHAPTER SIX

83 https://www.independent.co.uk/voices/mums-working-childcare-spring-budget-tories-b2294184.html
84 https://pregnantthenscrewed.com/press-release-mothers-have-had-enough-uk-protest-of-15000-sweeps-the-nation-to-demand-government-reforms-for-families/

85 https://pregnantthenscrewed.com/6-in-10-women-who-have-had-an-abortion-claim-childcare-costs-influenced-their

86 https://pregnantthenscrewed.com/three-quarters-of-mothers-who-pay-for-childcare-say-that-it-does-not-make-financial-sense-for-them-to-work/

87 https://www.independent.co.uk/news/uk/home-news/sarah-solemani-march-mummies-childcare-b2212731.html

88 https://www.earlyyearseducator.co.uk/features/article/sector-update-where-next-for-early-years-funding-affordability-and-the-budget

89 https://www.emwllp.com/latest/less-than-a-third-of-men-take-paternity-leave/ https://www.ucl.ac.uk/ioe/news/2021/sep/uks-parental-leave-policy-falls-short-its-european-counterparts

90 https://www.mumsnet.com/news/mega-survey-of-uk-parents-shows-that-child-care-is-failing-families

91 https://www.ons.gov.uk/peoplepopulationandcommunity/birthsdeathsand marriages/families/bulletins/familiesandhouseholds/2022

92 https://www.bbc.co.uk/news/education-64865602

93 https://www.coram.org.uk/news/coram-survey-finds-childcare-shortages-nationwide-with-the-most-disadvantaged-children-missing-out/

94 https://www.pwc.co.uk/press-room/press-releases/cost-of-living-weighs-on-childcare-finds-pwc-research.html

95 https://www.equalityhumanrights.com/en/our-work/news/pregnancy-and-maternity-discrimination-forces-thousands-new-mothers-out-their-jobs

96 https://pregnantthenscrewed.com/three-quarters-of-mothers-who-pay-for-childcare-say-that-it-does-not-make-financial-sense-for-them-to-work/

97 https://www.americanprogress.org/article/americas-child-care-deserts-2018/ https://strongnation.s3.amazonaws.com/documents/1598/05d917e2-9618-4648-a0ee-1b35d17e2a4d.pdf, https://www.strongnation.org/articles/2038-122-billion-the-growing-annual-cost-of-the-infant-toddler-child-care-crisis

98 https://www.eyalliance.org.uk/news/2021/06/new-data-shows-ministers-knew-early-years-was-underfunded

CHAPTER SEVEN

99 https://mappingpoliceviolence.org/

100 https://policeviolencereport.org/

101 https://www.met.police.uk/SysSiteAssets/media/downloads/met/about-us/baroness-casey-review/update-march-2023/baroness-casey-review-march-2023a.pdf

102 https://www.met.police.uk/SysSiteAssets/media/downloads/met/about-us/baroness-casey-review/baroness-casey-review-interim-report-on-misconduct.pdf

103 https://www.independent.co.uk/news/uk/home-news/police-sexual-misconduct-complaints-bullying-b1999688.html

104 https://assets.publishing.service.gov.uk/government/uploads/system/uploads/attachment_data/file/277111/4262.pdf

105 https://www.centreforwomensjustice.org.uk/news/2020/3/9/police-officers-allowed-to-abuse-with-impunity-in-the-locker-room-culture-of-uk-forces-super-complaint-reveals

106 https://www.independent.co.uk/news/uk/home-news/hmic-police-report-wayne-couzens-b2215382.html

107 https://www.inquest.org.uk/police-racism-report-2023
108 https://www.met.police.uk/SysSiteAssets/media/downloads/met/about-us/
baroness-casey-review/update-march-2023/baroness-casey-review-march-
2023a.pdf
109 https://www.independent.co.uk/news/uk/home-news/domestic-abuse-police-
black-and-ethnic-minority-b2236980.html
110 https://www.inquest.org.uk/bame-deaths-in-police-custody
111 https://assets.childrenscommissioner.gov.uk/wpuploads/2023/03/cc-strip-
search-of-children-in-england-and-wales.pdf

CHAPTER EIGHT

112 https://www.psychiatry.org/news-room/apa-blogs/chronic-pain-and-mental-
health-interconnected
113 https://www.ucl.ac.uk/news/2021/apr/analysis-womens-pain-routinely-under-
estimated-and-gender-stereotypes-are-blame
114 https://www.health.harvard.edu/blog/women-and-pain-disparities-in-
experience-and-treatment-2017100912562
115 https://www.nature.com/immersive/d41586-023-01475-2/index.html
116 https://assets.publishing.service.gov.uk/government/uploads/system/uploads/
attachment_data/file/1100721/Womens-Health-Strategy-England-web-
accessible.pdf
117 https://www.immdsreview.org.uk/downloads/IMMDSReview_Web.pdf
118 Ibid.
119 Ibid.
120 https://www.gov.uk/government/publications/final-report-of-the-ockenden-
review
121 Mother and Babies: Reducing Risk through Audits and Confidential Enquiries
across the UK
122 https://www.npeu.ox.ac.uk/mbrrace-uk/presentations/saving-lives-improving-
mothers-care
123 https://www.independent.co.uk/voices/period-pain-is-officially-as-bad-as-a-
heart-attack-so-why-have-doctors-ignored-it-the-answer-is-simple-a6883831.
html
124 https://www.independent.co.uk/news/uk/home-news/adhd-women-
gender-differences-b1993364.html
125 https://www.who.int/health-topics/women-s-health
126 https://www.independent.co.uk/news/health/lgbt-women-nhs-health-
care-uk-barriers-discrimination-study-a9113381.html
127 https://www.endometriosis-uk.org/endometriosis-facts-and-figures
128 https://www.unicef.org/press-releases/malnutrition-mothers-soars-25-cent-
crisis-hit-countries-putting-women-and-newborn
129 https://www.rcog.org.uk/about-us/global-network/centre-for-womens-global-
health/gynaecological-health/
130 https://www.independent.co.uk/news/health/women-low-income-households-
health-care-b2268060.html
131 https://www.independent.co.uk/news/health/women-health-diagnosis-
delay-treatment-b2280080.html

CHAPTER NINE

132 https://www.unodc.org/unodc/en/press/releases/2018/November/home-the-most-dangerous-place-for-women-with-majority-of-female-homicide-victims-worldwide-killed-by-partners-or-family--unodc-study-says.html

133 https://www.independent.co.uk/news/uk/crime/women-joint-enterprise-prison-sentences-b1722700.html, https://www.mmu.ac.uk/news-and-events/news/story/13185/

134 https://www.independent.co.uk/news/uk/home-news/women-pointless-arrests-criminal-justice-system-b1848981.html

135 https://www.independent.co.uk/news/uk/home-news/women-criminal-records-disclosed-jobs-stigma-b1813043.html, https://unlock.org.uk/wp-content/uploads/misc/The-impact-of-criminal-records-on-women.pdf

136 https://assets.publishing.service.gov.uk/government/uploads/system/uploads/attachment_data/file/639261/bame-disproportionality-in-the-cjs.pdf

137 https://webarchive.nationalarchives.gov.uk/ukgwa/20130128112038, http://www.justice.gov.uk/publications/docs/corston-report-march-2007.pdf

138 https://www.ox.ac.uk/news/2018-01-30-safeguarding-children-when-sentencing-mothers

139 https://prisonreformtrust.org.uk/project/women-the-criminal-justice-system/

140 https://assets.publishing.service.gov.uk/government/uploads/system/uploads/attachment_data/file/1119965/statistics-on-women-and-the-criminal-justice-system-2021-.pdf

141 https://assets.publishing.service.gov.uk/government/uploads/system/uploads/attachment_data/file/1119965/statistics-on-women-and-the-criminal-justice-system-2021-.pdf

142 https://www.independent.co.uk/news/uk/home-news/women-pointless-arrests-criminal-justice-system-b1848981.html

143 https://assets.publishing.service.gov.uk/government/uploads/system/uploads/attachment_data/file/1119965/statistics-on-women-and-the-criminal-justice-system-2021-.pdf

144 https://www.independent.co.uk/news/uk/home-news/arrests-women-distress-domestic-abuse-b670314.html

145 https://publications.parliament.uk/pa/cm5803/cmselect/cmjust/265/report.html

146 https://www.independent.co.uk/news/uk/home-news/women-prisoners-brain-injuries-domestic-violence-a8764536.html

CHAPTER TEN

147 https://pubmed.ncbi.nlm.nih.gov/28213723/

148 https://www.theguardian.com/lifeandstyle/2020/nov/01/the-sole-function-of-the-clitoris-is-female-orgasm-is-that-why-its-ignored-by-medical-science

149 https://pubmed.ncbi.nlm.nih.gov/20480220/

150 https://pubmed.ncbi.nlm.nih.gov/28213723/

151 https://www.kcl.ac.uk/policy-institute/assets/social-attitudes-in-the-uk-and-beyond-pub01-116.pdf

152 Ibid.

153 https://yougov.co.uk/topics/health/articles-reports/2019/03/08/half-brits-
dont-know-where-vagina-and-its-not-just
154 https://www.forbes.com/sites/alicebroster/2020/07/31/what-is-the-
orgasm-gap
155 Ibid.
156 https://yougov.co.uk/topics/health/articles-reports/2019/03/08/half-brits-
dont-know-where-vagina-and-its-not-just
157 https://www.cosmopolitan.com/uk/love-sex/sex/a43351077/how-ann-
summers-took-female-pleasure-mainstream/

CHAPTER ELEVEN

158 https://www.independent.co.uk/life-style/love-island-jessie-olivia-toxic-
femininity-b2298239.html
159 https://www.independent.co.uk/news/world/europe/toxic-masculinity-
france-road-deaths-b2278057.html
160 https://www.ncbi.nlm.nih.gov/pmc/articles/PMC5868426/
161 https://www.theatlantic.com/health/archive/2019/02/toxic-masculinity-
history/583411/
162 https://www.npr.org/2021/03/27/981803154/why-nearly-all-mass-shooters-
are-men, https://www.theviolenceproject.org/?s=98%25
163 https://www.independent.co.uk/news/uk/home-news/andrew-tate-
influence-young-men-misogyny-b2283595.html
164 Ibid.
165 https://futuremen.org/future-men-2018-survey/
166 https://stem4.org.uk/wp-content/uploads/2021/11/Toxic-masculinity-
stopping-boys-seeking-mental-health-support-survey-finds-Nov-21.pdf
167 https://www3.paho.org/hq/index.php?option=com_content&view=
article&id=15599

CHAPTER TWELVE

168 https://www.theguardian.com/society/2022/jun/16/rape-courts-pilot-in-
england-dismissed-as-gimmick-amid-low-conviction-rates
169 https://rapecrisis.org.uk/get-informed/statistics-sexual-violence/
170 https://assets.publishing.service.gov.uk/government/uploads/system/uploads/
attachment_data/file/1001417/end-to-end-rape-review-report-with-correction-
slip.pdf
171 https://rapecrisis.org.uk/get-informed/statistics-sexual-violence/
172 Ibid.
173 https://www.independent.co.uk/news/uk/home-news/women-police-sexual-
violence-crimes-b2299751.html
174 https://www.independent.co.uk/news/uk/home-news/rape-cases-court-
backlogs-delays-b2306706.html
175 https://rapecrisis.org.uk/news/new-report-reveals-the-devastating-
impact-of-the-crown-court-crisis-on-sexual-violence-survivors/
176 https://www.independent.co.uk/news/uk/home-news/rape-cases-court-
backlogs-delays-b2306706.html

177 https://www.independent.co.uk/news/uk/home-news/court-backlogs-covid-recovery-justice-b2080233.html

178 https://www.independent.co.uk/asia/south-asia/sexual-violence-south-asia-rape-b1833944.html

179 https://www.who.int/news-room/fact-sheets/detail/violence-against-women

180 https://www.unwomenuk.org/site/wp-content/uploads/2021/03/APPG-UN-Women-Sexual-Harassment-Report_Updated.pdf

181 https://plan-uk.org/media-centre/35-per-cent-of-girls-in-school-uniform-have-been-sexually-harassed-in-public-new-survey

182 https://www.cantbuymysilence.com/nda-info

183 https://www.speakoutrevolution.co.uk/the-speak-out-blogs/vsllc12tng5vff83uqilxgn7uyrxaj

184 https://rapecrisis.org.uk/get-informed/statistics-sexual-violence/

185 Ibid.

186 https://www.independent.co.uk/news/uk/crime/police-super-complaint-domestic-violence-sexual-violence-centre-for-women-s-justice-a8830366.html

187 Ibid.

188 https://rapecrisis.org.uk/news/new-crown-prosecution-service-guidance-will-block-rape-victims-from-therapy/

189 https://www.independent.co.uk/news/uk/home-news/rape-investigations-police-victim-blaming-b2245885.html

190 https://www.independent.co.uk/news/uk/home-news/sexual-harassment-teenage-girls-vawg-strategy-b1888073.html

191 https://www.who.int/news-room/fact-sheets/detail/violence-against-women

CHAPTER THIRTEEN

192 https://pubmed.ncbi.nlm.nih.gov/14686459/

193 https://www.manchester.ac.uk/discover/news/borderline-personality-disorder-has-strongest-link-to-childhood-trauma/

194 https://www.independent.co.uk/news/uk/home-news/mental-health-services-domestic-abuse-women-agenda-nhs-a9054371.html

195 https://assets.publishing.service.gov.uk/government/uploads/system/uploads/attachment_data/file/556596/apms-2014-full-rpt.pdf

196 https://www.independent.co.uk/news/uk/home-news/psychiatric-units-women-drugs-chemical-restraint-b2049272.html

197 https://www.independent.co.uk/news/health/electroconvulsive-therapy-brain-mental-health-b2095155.html

198 https://www.who.int/health-topics/depression

199 https://www.ncbi.nlm.nih.gov/pmc/articles/PMC4478054/
https://www.ncbi.nlm.nih.gov/pmc/articles/PMC5632782/
https://www.ncbi.nlm.nih.gov/pmc/articles/PMC3135672/
https://www.ncbi.nlm.nih.gov/pmc/articles/PMC3115767/

200 https://www.mentalhealth.org.uk/explore-mental-health/statistics/men-women-statistics

201 https://www.manchester.ac.uk/discover/news/steep-rise-in-self-harm-among-teenage-girls/

202 https://www.agendaalliance.org/our-work/projects-and-campaigns/womens-mental-health-facts/

203 https://bjgp.org/content/72/720/e511

204 https://www.independent.co.uk/news/uk/home-news/benzodiazepines-more-women-prescribed-than-men-b2184230.html

205 https://www.bbc.com/future/article/20190313-why-more-men-kill-themselves-than-women

206 https://onlinelibrary.wiley.com/doi/full/10.1111/inm.12873
https://labourlist.org/2020/10/new-data-alarming-as-black-people-four-times-more-likely-to-be-sectioned/

207 https://www.mentalhealth.org.uk/explore-mental-health/a-z-topics/men-and-mental-health

208 https://www.independent.co.uk/news/uk/home-news/women-drug-addiction-services-intimidating-b1973631.html

209 https://www.independent.co.uk/news/uk/home-news/domestic-abuse-link-suicide-women-b2286788.html

210 https://www.who.int/news/item/19-09-2022-launch-of-the-who-guide-for-integration-of-perinatal-mental-health

CHAPTER FOURTEEN

211 https://www.independent.co.uk/news/uk/home-news/sex-work-report-home-office-austerity-criminalisation-a9178146.html

212 https://www.independent.co.uk/news/uk/home-news/coronavirus-sex-work-prostitution-homeless-a9432846.html

213 https://essl.leeds.ac.uk/sociology/news/article/637/survey-by-dr-teela-sanders-reveals-previous-professions-of-sex-workers

214 https://www.independent.co.uk/news/uk/home-news/sex-work-cost-of-living-crisis-dangerous-clients-b2222507.html

215 https://academic.oup.com/aje/article/159/8/778/91471 / https://journals.sagepub.com/doi/10.1177/1088767918754306

216 Revolting Prostitutes: The Fight for Sex Workers' Rights, Juno Mac and Molly Smith

217 https://rewirenewsgroup.com/2011/06/29/louisiana-workers-will-longer-labeled-offenders-0/

218 https://www.independent.co.uk/news/uk/home-news/sex-work-brexit-vote-violence-deportation-threats-b1850271.html

219 https://www.independent.co.uk/news/uk/home-news/sex-work-trafficking-victims-raids-police-b2244505.html

220 https://s3.eu-west-3.amazonaws.com/observatoirebdd/2014_Violence_against_sex_workers_UK_Executive_Summary_CONNELLY_NUM_ENG.pdf

221 https://www.independent.co.uk/news/uk/home-news/sex-worker-rights-decriminalisation-law-reform-brothels-uk-a9076731.html

222 Revolting Prostitutes: The Fight for Sex Workers' Rights, Juno Mac and Molly Smith

223 https://www.amnestyusa.org/from-margin-to-center-sex-work-decriminalization-is-a-racial-justice-issue/

224 https://uglymugs.ie/wp-content/uploads/um-statement-26-mar-2019.pdf

CHAPTER FIFTEEN

225 https://prisonreformtrust.org.uk/too-many-women-sent-to-prison-on-short-sentences-for-non-violent-offences/

226 https://www.dailymail.co.uk/news/article-10491975/BBC-probe-sexist-licence-fee-convictions.html

227 https://www.gov.uk/government/statistics/women-and-the-criminal-justice-system-2021/women-and-the-criminal-justice-system-2021

228 https://www.independent.co.uk/news/uk/home-news/women-criminal-records-disclosed-jobs-stigma-b1813043.html

229 https://www.clinks.org/our-work/women-criminal-justice-system

230 Ibid.

231 Ibid.

232 https://www.prisonstudies.org/sites/default/files/resources/downloads/world_female_imprisonment_list_5th_edition.pdf

233 https://idpc.net/news/2022/10/world-female-prison-population-up-by-60-since-2000

234 https://www.independent.co.uk/news/uk/home-news/prison-spending-england-wales-europe-russia-b1828396.html, https://wp.unil.ch/space/files/2021/04/210330_FinalReport_SPACE_I_2020.pdf

235 https://www.independent.co.uk/news/uk/home-news/prisons-pregnant-women-remand-children-b1970551.html

236 https://www.nuffieldtrust.org.uk/sites/default/files/2020-02/prisoners-use-of-hospital-services-main-report.pdf

237 https://www.gov.uk/government/news/secretary-of-state-launches-dedicated-strategy-to-break-the-cycle-of-female-offending.

238 https://www.russellwebster.com/10-things-you-should-know-about-women-and-the-criminal-justice-system/
https://assets.publishing.service.gov.uk/government/uploads/system/uploads/attachment_data/file/1119965/statistics-on-women-and-the-criminal-justice-system-2021-.pdf

239 https://prisonreformtrust.org.uk/project/women-the-criminal-justice-system/

240 https://assets.publishing.service.gov.uk/government/uploads/system/uploads/attachment_data/file/1119965/statistics-on-women-and-the-criminal-justice-system-2021-.pdf

241 https://prisonreformtrust.org.uk/project/women-the-criminal-justice-system/

242 https://www.tommys.org/about-us/news-views/pregnant-women-prison-greater-risk-pregnancy-complications-and-baby-loss.

243 Ibid.

244 https://www.gov.uk/government/statistics/women-and-the-criminal-justice-system-2021/women-and-the-criminal-justice-system-2021

245 https://www.prisonpolicy.org/reports/pie2023.html

246 https://www.sentencingproject.org/fact-sheet/incarcerated-women-and-girls/

247 Ibid.

248 Ibid.

249 Ibid.

CHAPTER SIXTEEN

250 https://www.independent.co.uk/news/uk/home-news/women-body-image-anxiety-teenagers-international-day-of-the-girl-a9150956.html
251 https://www.beateatingdisorders.org.uk/get-information-and-support/about-eating-disorders/how-many-people-eating-disorder-uk/
252 https://www.thecalmzone.net/male-body-image
253 https://www.independent.co.uk/news/uk/home-news/eating-disorder-rise-pandemic-lockdown-b1798387.html
254 https://digital.nhs.uk/news/2020/nearly-one-in-five-women-screened-positive-for-possible-eating-disorder
255 https://www.independent.co.uk/news/uk/home-news/eating-disorders-lgbt-young-people-b1844881.html
256 https://bmcpsychiatry.biomedcentral.com/articles/10.1186/s12888-020-2433-8
257 https://www.independent.co.uk/news/health/children-eating-disorder-waits-b2077575.html
258 https://www.independent.co.uk/news/uk/home-news/bmi-eating-disorders-body-image-b1828537.html, https://committees.parliament.uk/committee/328/women-and-equalities-committee/news/153711/government-approach-to-negative-body-image-dangerous/
259 https://www.mentalhealth.org.uk/explore-mental-health/articles/body-image-report-executive-summary
260 Ibid.
261 Ibid.
262 https://yougov.co.uk/topics/health/articles-reports/2021/08/05/yougov-body-image-study
263 https://www.independent.co.uk/independentpremium/uk-news/drunkorexia-health-effects-alcohol-eating-disorder-a9527221.html, https://www.unisa.edu.au/Media-Centre/Releases/2020/binge-drinkers-beware-drunkorexia-is-calling/
264 https://journals.sagepub.com/doi/abs/10.1177/1461444819826530?journalCode=nmsa

CHAPTER SEVENTEEN

265 https://www.youtube.com/watch?v=ROwquxC_Gxc
266 https://twitter.com/i/status/896032277062443009
267 https://autonomy.work/portfolio/jari/

CHAPTER EIGHTEEN

268 https://www.engage.england.nhs.uk/safety-and-innovation/menopause-in-the-workplace/
269 https://www.independent.co.uk/independentpremium/menopausal-women-mental-health-b1864347.html

270 https://www.independent.co.uk/news/health/menopause-women-private-healthcare-b1868051.html
271 https://www.channel4.com/programmes/davina-mccall-sex-myths-and-the-menopause
272 https://www.who.int/news-room/fact-sheets/detail/menopause
273 https://www.rpharms.com/about-us/news/details/delay-to-prepayment-scheme-for-hrt-disappointing
274 https://doi.org/10.3399/bjgp20X713045
275 https://menopausesupport.co.uk/?p=14434
276 Ibid.
277 https://insightplus.bakermckenzie.com/bm/employment-compensation/united-kingdom-menopause-a-business-issue
278 https://www.independent.co.uk/news/uk/home-news/menopause-women-leaving-work-b2132663.html
279 https://www.fawcettsociety.org.uk/menopauseandtheworkplace
280 https://doi.org/10.1186/s40695-022-00073-y
281 https://www.ipsos.com/sites/default/files/ct/news/documents/2022-11/Almost%20a%20quarter%20of%20the%20worlds%20women%20are%20not%20comfortable%20talking%20about%20menopause%20_Ipsos_Press%20Release_10%20November%202022.pdf
282 https://www.who.int/news-room/fact-sheets/detail/menopause

CHAPTER NINETEEN

283 https://www.reuters.com/article/us-britain-women-honourviolence-idUSKBN1K31X4
284 https://journals.sagepub.com/doi/full/10.1177/1077801220952168
285 https://www.unicef.org/press-releases/2-million-additional-cases-female-genital-mutilation-likely-occur-over-next-decade
286 Ibid.
287 https://www.independent.co.uk/news/uk/home-news/honour-crimes-women-fgm-murder-abuse-convictions-cps-a9001321.html
288 https://www.theguardian.com/society/2021/oct/31/honour-based-offences-soared-by-81-in-last-five-years
289 https://safelives.org.uk/sites/default/files/resources/Spotlight%20on%20HBV%20and%20forced%20marriage-web.pdf
290 https://www.cps.gov.uk/sites/default/files/documents/publications/cps_vawg_report_2016.pdf
291 https://www.independent.co.uk/news/uk/home-news/honour-based-abuse-reports-surge-coronavirus-lockdown-forced-marriage-a9516311.html
292 https://www.justiceinspectorates.gov.uk/hmicfrs/news/news-feed/every-police-force-must-improve-its-understanding-of-hbv/
293 https://www.forwarduk.org.uk/violence-against-women-and-girls/female-genital-mutilation/
294 https://www.unicef.org/protection/female-genital-mutilation
295 https://hbv-awareness.com/statistics-data/
296 https://link.springer.com/chapter/10.1007/978-3-030-55985-4_17

CHAPTER TWENTY

297 https://www.independent.co.uk/news/uk/home-news/ons-trans-gender-data-uk-b2257199.html
298 https://www.ipso.co.uk/news-press-releases/press-releases/
new-research-on-reporting-of-trans-issues-shows-400-increase-in-coverage-and-varying-perceptions-on-broader-editorial-standards/
299 https://www.independent.co.uk/news/uk/crime/hate-crime-transgender-uk-figures-b2196759.html
300 https://link.springer.com/article/10.1007/s13178-018-0335-z
301 https://static1.squarespace.com/static/5e8a0a6bb02c73725b24dc9d/t/6152ea
c81e0b0109491dc518/1632824024793/Trans+Lives+Survey+2021.pdf
302 https://www.stonewall.org.uk/system/files/lgbt_in_britain_work_report.pdf
303 https://www.stonewall.org.uk/system/files/lgbt_in_britain_hate_crime.pdf
304 https://ilga.org/state-sponsored-homophobia-report-2020-global-legislation-overview
305 https://ilga.org/downloads/ILGA_World_State_Sponsored_Homophobia_
report_global_legislation_overview_update_December_2020.pdf
306 https://www.stonewall.org.uk/our-work/campaigns/campaigning-global-lgbt-equality
307 https://www.unesco.org/en/articles/report-shows-homophobic-and-transphobic-violence-education-be-global-problem
308 https://www.independent.co.uk/news/world/americas/gay-transgender-women-cancer-risk-heterosexual-lgbt-a8921831.html
309 https://transrespect.org/en/tmm-update-tdor-2022/

CHAPTER TWENTY ONE

310 https://refuge.org.uk/news/refuge-publishes-data-showing-charging-rates-remain-woefully-low-on-intimate-image-abuse/
311 https://www.nytimes.com/2018/09/03/world/asia/korea-toilet-camera.html
312 https://www.hrw.org/report/2021/06/16/my-life-not-your-porn/digital-sex-crimes-south-korea
313 https://www.independent.co.uk/news/uk/home-news/girl-grooming-child-sex-abuse-livestreaming-internet-watch-a9300946.html
314 https://www.independent.co.uk/news/uk/home-news/revenge-porn-criminalise-threats-domestic-abuse-bill-b1791224.html
315 https://www.independent.co.uk/independentpremium/sex-revenge-porn-online-crime-extortion-victims-a9478866.html
316 https://revengepornhelpline.org.uk/resources/helpline-research-and-reports/revenge-porn-helpline-cases-and-trends-of-2021/
317 https://www.independent.co.uk/news/uk/england-wales-police-data-refuge-b2080235.html